GREENING CITIES, GROWING COMMUNITIES

26 in 26
Neighborhood Resource Centers
26 Neighborhood Strategies in a 26 month time frame
A Grant Funded by the LSTA
(Library Services & Technology Act)

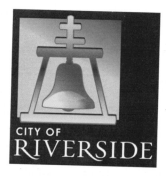

Riverside Public Library

GREENING CITIES, GROWING COMMUNITIES

Learning from Seattle's Urban Community Gardens

JEFFREY HOU, JULIE M. JOHNSON, and LAURA J. LAWSON

Landscape Architecture Foundation, Washington, D.C. *in association with*

University of Washington Press, Seattle & London

University of Washington Press

P.O. Box 50096, Seattle, WA 98145, U.S.A.

www.washington.edu/uwpress

Landscape Architecture Foundation

818 18th Street NW, Suite 810, Washington, DC 20006

Library of Congress Cataloging-in-Publication Data

Hou, Jeffrey, 1967–

Greening cities, growing communities : urban
community gardens in Seattle /
Jeffrey Hou, Julie Johnson, and Laura Lawson.

p. cm.

Includes bibliographical references and index.

ISBN 978-0-295-98928-0 (cloth : alk. paper)

1. Community gardens—Washington (State)—Seattle.
2. Urban gardening—
Washington (State)—Seattle. I. Johnson, Julie, 1962–
II. Lawson, Laura. III. Title.

SB457.3.H63 2009

635.091732—dc22   2009005341

The paper used in this publication is acid-free and
90 percent recycled from at least 50 percent post-
consumer waste. It meets the minimum requirements
of American National Standard for Information
Sciences—Permanence of Paper for Printed Library
Materials, ANSI z39.48-1984.

ADDITIONAL PHOTO CREDITS

Inside cover: High Point's market garden
is framed by this colorful fence, created
by residents and Mithun architects while
designing the new community. Photograph by
Juan Hernandez, 2006. Courtesy of Mithun.

p. ii: Sunflowers thrive in High Point's large
community garden, sending a message of
welcome to the surrounding neighborhood.
Photograph by Juan Hernandez, 2008.
Courtesy of Mithun.

p. 2: Native drought-tolerant and site-
suitable plants minimize irrigation, pesticide
use, and storm water runoff at High Point
Community. Photograph by Juan Hernandez,
2008. Courtesy of Mithun.

p. x: Photograph by Ashley Saleeba, 2008.

p. 62: Photograph by Ashley Saleeba, 2008.

p. 198: Photograph by Ashley Saleeba, 2008.

CONTENTS

PART II SEATTLE CASE STUDIES

PART III LESSONS FROM SEATTLE

ACKNOWLEDGMENTS

This case study was conducted under the auspices of the Landscape Architecture Foundation as part of their ongoing support for case-study research aimed at furthering the academic and professional knowledge of the profession. We are grateful for the Foundation's support of this research, and the direction provided by Susan Everett, Executive Director of the Landscape Architecture Foundation, and the LAF staff.

Our accumulated knowledge of Seattle's community gardens was only possible because of the enthusiastic support of Seattle's community gardeners and the staff at P-Patch, P-Patch Trust, the Department of Neighborhoods, and other organizations. Thank you to Jim Diers, former director of the Department of Neighborhoods, for sharing historic and personal accounts. We appreciate the openness of Rich MacDonald, Barbara Donnette, and P-Patch Program staff members. We are grateful to garden activists such as Susan Casey, Joyce Moty, and Ray Shutte for assisting us in the early phase of the research. Danny Stratten, Leslie Morishita, and Jennifer Brower of Inter*Im assisted us with research on the Danny Woo Community Garden. Yao-Fou Chao assisted us in interviewing the Mien gardeners.

This collaborative effort was facilitated by the support provided by our two institutions: the Department of Landscape Architecture at the University of Washington and the Department of Landscape Architecture at the University of Illinois, Urbana-Champaign. Particularly, the support from the Johnston/Hasting Publication Endowment at the College of Built Environments, University of Washington was critical to the final production of the manuscript. We are grateful to Chair Fritz Wagner and administrator Vicky Reyes for their assistance and support for this project.

Much of the fieldwork was conducted by our superb research assistants, Vanessa Lee, Arielle Farina Clark, and Diana Yuen. Nathan Brightbill, Nicholas Brown, Leslie Gia Clark, Sungkyung Lee, and Danielle Pierce assisted in the final production.

We appreciate the insights given by our initial reviewers who helped us see ways to organize the information and make it most useful to academics, practitioners, and officials. Thank you to Stan Jones and Daniel Winterbottom. We are grateful to our editor, Kerrie Maynes, for her attention and support during the final stages of production.

Lastly, we thank our families for their support and encouragement. We hope this book honors the memory of Virginia Huse (1919-2006) who enjoyed a very full life in Seattle.

GREENING CITIES, GROWING COMMUNITIES

A Case for Urban Community Gardens as Public Open Space

The urban community garden is generally regarded as a model of community open space that provides multiple environmental, social, economic, and health benefits. Community gardens have been started by local residents seeking an alternative form of open space, by institutions that use gardening to fulfill programmatic functions such as job training and horticultural therapy, and by public agencies that consider gardening on a par with sports and other forms of public recreation. For the people who are involved in creating or maintaining a garden, satisfaction can be found in the tangible transformation of a site, the productivity of cultivation and the resulting nutrition, the fulfillment of community open-space needs, meeting neighbors and working together, and fostering a more sustainable and healthy community. While participating gardeners realize many personal benefits, ranging from food to recreation and socialization, community gardens are also of interest to others who may enjoy passing by a garden or attending a garden tour, harvest fair, or educational workshop.

Numerous studies and reports praise and promote the community garden as a beneficial resource in communities, yet our full understanding of the issues involved in making and sustaining community gardens has lagged behind this appreciation. Cultivated by many different hands and evolving over time, a community garden is a distinct form of open space that reflects the many participants engaged in its creation and maintenance. Individuals often start a garden opportunistically—cultivating an otherwise underused plot of private or public land—yet this does not mean that the activists intend the garden to be temporary. Hundreds of volunteer hours may be dedicated to garden development and upkeep. Given the labor involved in making a garden and participant reliance on them for recreation, food, and other needs, many gardeners intend their gardens to be permanent fixtures in their community, and so wish to be granted the same degree of public support and protection as are given to parks and other public services.

This perspective is somewhat at odds with general policy and land-use perception that places community gardens as temporary, user-driven projects that require minimal attention to their longer-term public function. The land on which gardens exist is often considered "vacant" even though the plants and structures on the site bear witness to the persistent stewardship provided by the gardeners. If zoned for another use, the garden may be viewed as a temporary placeholder until there is interest in developing it for a "higher and better use." Officials may support local gardening efforts because there is local demand, but that does not mean that they regard it in the same light as traditional recreational activities that are permanently provided, such as sports fields or playgrounds. There are many possible explanations for this perspective. First, when one thinks about the avocation of gardening, it is generally in the context of one's own residence, not public space. When this space is surrounded by a fence and the food grown is consumed by individuals, the public nature may be questioned. Second, when compared to other public spaces, such as parks and plazas, a community garden site—with its cacophony of plants, tomato cages, wheelbarrows, and paths—may look uncontrolled or unkempt, especially in the off-season. Third, community gardens' incremental and idiosyncratic nature often goes against traditional approaches to the management of public areas.

I.1
The Warrington Community Garden in West Philadelphia was started in 1973 on an abandoned lot. Amid development pressure, the gardeners worked with the Neighborhood Gardening Association (NGA), a Philadelphia-based land trust, to purchase the site, which they now lease from the NGA. Photograph by Vanessa Lee, 2007.

I.2
Community gardens often reflect the ethnic traditions of their gardeners, such as this casita garden in New York's Lower East Side, which is located on a vacant lot. Photograph by Vanessa Lee, 2007.

However, the combined individual, community, and environmental benefits associated with community gardens warrant a deeper look into what gardens provide, how they are structured, and what is necessary to sustain their beneficial capacities and unique characteristics.

While community gardens exist in many different contexts, this book focuses on urban community gardens. In this context, the community garden is understood in its potential to promote individual and community activity, connection, expression, and health in the urban environment. By describing the processes of development, maintenance, and participation involved in community gardening, the authors reveal layers of community engagement and public support as well as limitations that hinder efforts. Through a review of existing literature and case studies on contemporary gardens, this book provides a rich description of community gardens that synthesizes planning and design considerations with the personal, social, and community outcomes sought by participants. The resulting perspective reveals the capacity of urban community gardens to address more extensive urban issues, such as community food security; urban ecosystem health; active living; pedestrian-friendly neighborhoods and open-space networks; and the equity concerns of low-income and minority communities, immigrants, and seniors. The ability of community gardens to improve such a range of urban concerns has implications for urban sustainability in all of its social, economic, and environmental dimensions. The case studies included in this book provide opportunities to see how broad concepts of sustainability are actually reflected in tangible actions and physical site design. The book concludes with a vision of urban community gardens as hybrid public spaces that serve a range of spatial and social needs at telescoping scales of site, neighborhood, community, and city. A series of lessons and steps emerges that suggests actions by gardeners, designers and planners, not-for-profit organizations, researchers and educators, city officials and agencies, and citizens at large.

LEARNING FROM SEATTLE

To demonstrate how community gardens can be legitimate and permanent land uses in cities, it is important to look at current examples in which community

I.3
When surrounded by tall corn and other crops, it is hard to imagine that the Watts Growing Project is located in a busy industrial and residential neighborhood of Los Angeles. Photograph by Lewis Watts, 2001.

gardens are recognized and supported as part of urban open-space planning and programming. In cities throughout North America, gardening organizations, parks and recreation departments, and allied interests are securing gardens. The flourishing gardens in many cities testify to supportive partnerships and interagency coordination that provide garden groups with garden sites, materials, technical assistance, and more. However, only a few cities include community gardens as open space in their city-planning process, and even fewer provide a protective zoning classification. For the purpose of this investigation, we chose Seattle specifically to look at how urban community gardens contribute to a system of urban open space, what persistent challenges emerge, and how these gardens are supported through a web of community activism, professional practice, and institutional mechanisms. While the conditions and experiences in Seattle may be unique, we believe Seattle's programs offer insights and lessons for other cities and communities. Given the wide range of community gardens, participants, and supporting institutions and agencies, this study offers broad implications for understanding the diverse roles of urban community gardens and productive partnerships among the different actors, organizations, and institutions.

APPROACH TO RESEARCH

As part of the Landscape Architecture Foundation's Land and Community Design Case Study Series, this research is intended to provide both a rich description of an innovative landscape type—the urban community garden—as well as a critical analysis that raises awareness of the concerns, opportunities, and challenges faced in their creation and sustainability. The case-study method requires gathering information from many different sources in order to address historical context, site considerations, participant perspectives, financial aspects, development processes, and other considerations (Francis 1999). This is a place-based study that focuses on six gardens located in the City of Seattle. While framing the discussion within a broader context of urban community gardens in general, the six cases allow for in-depth discussion of how sites, users, partnering organizations and agencies, funding, and other factors influenced the resulting unique places. The tension between generalities and specific situations reinforces the reality that urban community gardens are a common land-use type in need of deeper understanding while also being very particular and idiosyncratic as a result of locale and participation.

To identify relevant issues, this research includes a brief historical overview of community gardens in the United States, categorization and review of relevant literature from an array of disciplines, and a discussion of the functions community gardens serve. For the case studies of Seattle's community gardens, the research team conducted archival research and interviewed community garden activists, gardeners, and city staff to understand the specific history and evolution of community gardens in Seattle. Specific gardens were selected to provide examples of context, design approach, participation, and evolution. Interviews with participants provided narrative accounts of how individuals were involved in place making. Certain dimensions were particularly important:

- gardens implemented through community-engaged, volunteer-driven processes
- gardens that serve as resources for low-income communities, immigrants, and seniors
- gardens that serve public functions as part of parks and public open space
- gardens that display unique art and design features
- gardens that have evolved over many years (thirty or more)
- gardens that include educational and outreach programs
- gardens that demonstrate sustainable gardening and building practices
- gardens that create native plant habitats
- gardens located in communities with changing demographics as a result of immigration and/or gentrification

The selected case studies are not intended to be replicable models but instead reveal the breadth of types and issues that shape community gardens. The socio-economic and physical context, participants, priorities, opportunities, external supports, and evolution shape what each garden accomplishes. Our analysis across these gardens draws out lessons of how urban community gardens afford multiple expressions of urban sustainability and confront persistent challenges. Our conclusions suggest approaches to designing gardens as hybrid public spaces and present visions of urban community gardens serving individuals and families, neighborhoods, communities and districts, cities, and coalitions, with recommended actions to achieve these visions.

Table I.1.
Case study in land and community design: Urban community gardens

ISSUE NAME	Community gardens
LANDSCAPE TYPE	Urban open space
ISSUE SIGNIFICANCE AND IMPACT	Participation, context, and public policy affect the design, planning, programs, and sustainability of urban community gardens (working definition)
LESSONS LEARNED	1. Community gardens take many forms in response to site, people, and program. 2. Sustaining community gardens requires attention to participation and public support. 3. Participants seek a range of benefits that, in turn, determine the form, programming, and other factors of the garden. 4. Public policies and resources are critical to the sustainability of community gardens. 5. Planners, designers, and policy makers influence the sustainability of gardens through both site-specific involvement and citywide policies. 6. Most community gardens develop incrementally over time and evolve in response to community change, participant priorities, and opportunities that arise. 7. Community gardens offer multidimensional amenities that are important to the health and social and environmental well-being of individuals, communities, and cities.
CONTACTS	Seattle P-Patch Program P-Patch Trust / Friends of P-Patch American Community Gardening Association Trust for Public Land
KEYWORDS	open space, gardening, food security, recreation, community revitalization, urban sustainability

PART I

UNDERSTANDING URBAN COMMUNITY GARDENS

The challenge of describing community gardens is that they are simultaneously a simple concept—a place devoted to gardening—and a complicated social process shaped by participant dynamics, environment, political context, and more. Community gardens exist in most American cities, and while they share some common attributes, each garden is also unique because of its participants, site, and urban context. Part 1 of this book provides a general description of community gardens in order to inform a more specific analysis of gardens in Seattle.

Chapter 1 provides an overview of urban community gardens. A brief historical account reveals that urban community gardening has been a persistent though minor theme in urban development since the 1890s. An overview of literature and research on community gardens distinguishes different ways that community gardens have been documented and analyzed, including "how-to" books, narrative and descriptive texts, academic study related to a range of disciplines, and literature directly related to planning and design issues. This review sets the context for a general discussion of the roles and resources urban community gardens provide through their physical presence in a community; the social interaction necessary for design, development, and maintenance of community gardens; and the educational and programmatic elements often included. The capacity of urban community gardens to address such a wide range of social and environmental concerns implicates them in a holistic concept of urban sustainability that touches on household everyday needs as well as neighborhood and community activism and place making.

Chapter 2 describes the general process of creating and sustaining a community garden. While each community garden is shaped by its particular context of site, participation, and community, there are some general considerations that all community gardens must address. These include initial conception, site selection, planning and design process, implementation and maintenance, participation and leadership, evolution, and relationship to citywide planning.

Chapter 3 provides a description of the Seattle context in preparation for the case studies that follow. Descriptions of Seattle's environmental conditions, urban history, and demographic change, as well as the legacy of civic activism, serve as a basis for understanding the history of urban community gardening in the city. This chapter also summarizes some of the key organizations that have supported the community gardening movement in Seattle and continue to shape its evolution into the future.

1

Community Gardens in America

Linking two powerful concepts—community and garden—elicits a wide range of meanings based on a person's experience, expectations, and outlook. The term "community garden" is probably best understood as a defined area of tillable land made available to groups of individuals, households, classes, and others to garden. Within this broad definition, the size, location, age, participation, and programmatic elements of a community garden can vary widely, from a small garden in New York's Battery Park City to a four-acre garden in California's Hollywood Hills. While the focus is often on cultivation of vegetables, fruits, and herbs for consumption, community gardens may also include flowers, orchards, theme gardens, educational areas, playgrounds, and lawn areas for relaxation and play. Often, community gardens are created on vacant land in neighborhoods, but they can also be found in parks, on hospital and jail grounds, in housing developments, and even at places of work. Many gardens are started by individuals who personally seek a place to garden, but others are initiated by schools, nonprofit organizations, and public agencies that consider the programmatic potential of gardening as beneficial to their constituencies. In general, participation is voluntary, although some programs that involve employment, training, or therapy may require some degree of enrollment or accountability.

Called many names—community gardens, allotment gardens, vacant-lot gardens, neighborhood gardens, rent-a-garden, and garden patches—these gardens share the basic component of providing a shared place for people to garden.

1.1
The Liberty Community Garden in Lower Manhattan provides a small space to garden amid apartment towers. Located close to the World Trade Center site, the garden provided a means for Seattle's gardeners to express their sorrow and hope by sending a cubic yard of compost made from flowers collected at a Seattle vigil for victims of September 11, 2001. Photograph by Laura Lawson, 1999.

1.2
Located in the Hollywood Hills, the Wattles Farm and Neighborhood Garden was started in 1975 with thirty members and has since grown to include 169 garden plots, each measuring approximately fifteen feet square. Photograph by Lewis Watts, 2001.

Acknowledging the many forms and positive results possible with community gardens, the American Community Gardening Association (ACGA) has put forward the inclusive concept of "community greening." As described by Marc Breslav (1991), greening is "the intentional, beneficial activity by which plants, through

assistance or benign neglect by people, are encouraged to return or thrive within or near any area of human settlement, and thereby encourage feelings of empowerment, connectedness, and common concern among the settlement's human residents and visitors." Because many community gardens not only provide gardening space for individuals but also include programmatic elements, such as educational programs, job training, or community leadership development, Laura Lawson (2005) coined the term "urban garden program" to emphasize that objectives and programmed activities often determine participation and longevity. No matter what they are called, these gardens illustrate a desire to grow plants and participate in the care of a garden.

While interest has been building over the past few decades, community gardening has a much longer history in the United States, which can be traced back to the 1890s. As the nation has urbanized, many different programs have emerged to provide community gardens in cities. Phases of popularity include the vacant lot cultivation associations during the 1893–97 depression, the children's school garden movement from 1890 to 1920, civic gardening campaigns, World War I gardens, relief and subsistence garden programs during the 1930s depression, World War II victory gardens, and the current community gardening movement (Lawson 2005). Each phase is shaped by contemporary issues; some focus on gardening for nutrition and job training, others on neighborhood activism and beautification, and still others on environmental education and outreach. Most efforts to promote citywide or national programs tend to align with social or economic crises, with gardening considered to be a tangible and direct means to address concerns locally. As argued by historian Thomas Bassett (1981), community gardens serve as a coping strategy to

1.4
During World War I, community gardens such as this one in Cleveland were started on vacant lots, on industrial land, in public parks, and anywhere "slacker" land could be found. Reprinted from Charles Lathrop Pack, *War Garden Victorious* (Philadelphia: J. B. Lippincott Company, 1919).

1.5
During World War II, people gardened as part of the war effort. This victory garden was located in Forest Hills, Queens, New York. Photograph by Howard Hollem, U.S. Office of War Information. Courtesy of Library of Congress, LC-USW 3-42656D.

support cultural systems during times of social or economic crisis. During war, economic depression, or social unrest, people find satisfaction in becoming involved and seeing their effort transform bare earth into a productive garden. While the larger problem reaches beyond the control of individuals, an individual can make a difference in his or her own life and community by gardening.

1.6
Urban community gardens such as the Liz Christy Community Garden in New York City emerged as a result of local activism to address environmental, social, and economic concerns in the 1970s. This garden continues to provide an important open space for the city. Photograph by Laura Lawson, 2008.

Within this recurring effort to provide community gardens, there is variety in how programs have been implemented and sustained. Up until the 1960s, most garden programs were started by reformers, educators, and civic leaders who considered gardening to be a way to serve the broader population. Women's clubs, garden clubs, schools, and associations took on the task of acquiring land, hiring supervisors, and soliciting participation. Quite often, there were social or moral incentives that specifically targeted programs to new immigrants, the urban poor, and children, whom the organizers hoped to change as a result of their participation. While advocating for community gardens to address an immediate economic or social concern, leaders often hoped to arouse a love of gardening that would catalyze civic beautification, better health and nutrition, positive social interaction, and even the desire to become homeowners with private gardens (Lawson 2004). In the 1960s and 1970s, there was a shift to grassroots organizing based on neighborhood activism to address disinvestment, a new environmental ethic, inflation, and other concerns. Interest continued to grow, often with support from other institutions, including the federal United States Department of Agriculture's Urban Gardening Program, the ACGA, parks and recreation departments, and others. While past phases of garden promotion tended to fade away as popular attention diverted to other issues, current community garden activism tends to promote gardens as permanent community resources that provide a wide array of benefits to participants and neighborhoods.

Today, community gardens stand at the forefront of the community open space movement, which has expanded opportunities for recreation, socialization, and expression through local activism and user participation. Starting in the 1960s and 1970s, this movement grew out of increased frustration that traditional park facilities were not adequate in terms of location, program, and design, in part because local input was not obtained. Especially in urban neighborhoods characterized by depopulation and abandoned properties, neighbors took the initiative to reclaim vacant lots for positive activities, and in the process formed community ties that catalyzed greater community empowerment (Francis, Cashdan, and Paxson 1984; Hester 1984). In New York City, for instance, a 1984 inventory identified 448 community gardens and parks, totaling 155 acres and tended by 11,171 people (Fox, Koeppel, and Kellam 1985). Described by Mark Francis as an alternative park system, community open spaces are "neighborhood spaces designed, developed or managed by local residents on vacant land; may include viewing gardens, play areas, and community gardens; often developed on private land; not officially viewed as part of open space systems in cities; often vulnerable to displacement by other uses such as housing and commercial development" (Francis 1987, 78). While user initiation is fundamental to the community open space movement, many parks departments also have responded to new demands for recreation by supporting community efforts or creating new spaces such as tot lots, vest-pocket parks, adventure playgrounds, plazas, and community gardens (Cranz 1989).

Today, interest in community gardening is widespread. While there is no comprehensive data on the number of community gardens in the United States or the number of people involved in them, there are indicators of national distribution and interest. As of 1999, membership in the ACGA included over seven hundred organizations that represented over half a million people and almost every state. Its membership includes individual gardeners, neighborhood groups, citywide garden organizations, extension agents, educators, designers, planners, and social service providers. The most recent source for national data comes from a survey conducted by the ACGA in 1996 that includes results from thirty-six organizations in twenty-four cities. The data reflected the status of 6,020 gardens, which included mostly neighborhood gardens but also gardens located at schools, mental health and rehabilitation facilities, senior centers, and in other contexts. The survey found that the cities with the most gardens were New York (1,906 gardens), Newark (1,318), Philadelphia (1,135), Minneapolis (536), and Boston (148). While larger cities generally had more gardens, the cities with greater densities of gardens per population (per ten thousand residents) were Newark, Minneapolis, Philadelphia, Trenton, and Pittsburgh. The survey also showed a steady gain in the number of gardens, with over 2,000 new gardens—or a 35 percent increase over the previous five years. However, some cities also lost gardens—318 in total in the same five-year period. The survey revealed that each responding city had its own character in terms of garden longevity, support, advancement, and decline.

Table 1.1.

Top fifteen cities, ranked by number of gardens, in 1996 (ACGA Survey 1998)

	CITY	NUMBER OF GARDENS	POPULATION	GARDENS PER 10,000 RESIDENTS
1	New York	1,906	7,330,000	2.6
2	Newark	1,318	268,000	49.0
3	Philadelphia	1,135	1,552,000	7.3
4	Minneapolis	536	363,000	14.8
5	Boston	148	552,000	2.7
6	San Francisco	131	729,000	1.8
7	Pittsburgh	108	367,000	2.9
8	Houston	81	1,690,000	.48
9	Trenton	60	89,000	6.8
10	Washington, D.C.	58	607,000	1.3
11	Denver	54	484,000	1.1
12	Seattle	44	520,000	.87
13	New Orleans	43	490,000	.88
14	Spokane	42	187,000	2.2
15	Madison	37	195,000	1.9

RESEARCH AND LITERATURE ON COMMUNITY GARDENS

Because community gardens have been associated with a wide range of personal, social, and environmental benefits, they have been the focus of research and study in an array of disciplines. In some cases, the community garden has been studied as a physical site, while in others it is the social process that warrants study. To aid in deciphering the benefits associated with community gardens and the methods used to gather information, this overview is divided into four categories: "nuts and bolts" documentation, descriptive and narrative accounts from gardeners, research on benefits associated with community gardens, and community gardens as discussed in planning and design literature.

"Nuts and Bolts" Documentation

Since many community gardens are started by small community groups and organizations, sharing information about how to start and maintain a garden has been essential to the expansion of the movement. In the 1970s and 1980s, when community gardens were being developed in many communities as a way to address urban decay and inflation, a handful of books and articles were published to pass on practical advice to people who were interested in starting community gardens in new areas. Written for the layperson, these books provide information on plants and cultivation as well as organizational suggestions for acquiring land, coordinating volunteers, obtaining funds, and promoting community involvement. Quite often, descriptions of successful gardens evoked optimism about what was possible. One of the first books, *Gardens for All,* published by a group of the same name in 1973, described the impetus and procedures used for its own gardening program in Burlington, Vermont, as well as programs in Toronto; Boston; Ann Arbor; New York City; Santa Barbara; Asheville, North Carolina; and Appleton, Wisconsin. Mary Coe's 1978 book, *Growing with Community Gardening,* thoughtfully explored the impelling reasons why more people were engaging in community gardening and presented practical advice on site selection, organization, site planning, maintenance, and communication. Jamie Jobb's *The Complete Book of Community Gardening* (1979) described resources used by various communities to acquire land, volunteers, equipment, and funds. Based on successful efforts in Boston, the group Boston Urban Gardeners published *A Handbook of Community Gardening* (1982) that provided directions for organizing neighborhood gardens. Continuing in the effort to educate about community gardens, in 1984 Gardens for All and the National Association for Gardening published Larry Sommers's *The Community Garden Book,* with information on organizing, acquiring sites, getting funds, and potential program opportunities.

More recently, the ACGA has taken the lead in providing practical advice to existing and potential gardening groups on how to start and sustain a community garden. The ACGA provides useful information to practitioners/activists on its Web site and through its quarterly magazine and monographs. The ACGA's online resource, "Starting a Community Garden," includes information on site selection and preparation, insurance, setting up an organization and its bylaws, management, application procedures, and resources for materials and training. It also has developed the Growing Communities Curriculum, which includes advice on how to address diversity, asset-based community development, community organizing, leadership development, group decision making, developing a board of directors, fundraising strategies, and coalition planning, as well as other topics (Abi-Nader, Buckley, Dunnigan, and Markley, 2001). Because many ACGA members request hard data on benefits associated with community gardening to back up their lobbying and promotion efforts, the ACGA has encouraged and collaborated with research conducted by graduate students and universities, including case studies and citywide and national surveys (Aquino-Ramirez 1995; Monroe-Santos 1997; Hassan and Nur 1995).

In addition to the ACGA, there are supporting nonprofit organizations that provide resources for people interested in community gardens. The National Gardening Association (previously called Gardens for All) publishes useful information on gardening and is particularly supportive of children's gardening efforts. In many cities, cooperative extension, nonprofit organizations, and educational programs produce brochures and pamphlets that provide information on local resources, growing conditions, and other technical support.

Descriptive Accounts and Narratives from Gardeners

Many people learn about the experiential qualities of community gardening through publications that share stories of individual gardeners and their gardens. In *To Dwell Is to Garden* (1987), historian Sam Bass Warner and photographer Hansi Durlach weave together a history of community gardening in Boston with an exploration of cultural expression and personal portraits of gardeners. In *Transitory Gardens, Uprooted Lives* (1993), author Diane Balmori and photographer Margaret Morton highlight the capacity for community gardens to serve as sanctuaries and as a means of expression for New York's homeless people. Various community garden organizations have published accounts of their gardens and gardeners (Bloom and Bromberg 2004; Halverson and Flint 2005; Landman 1993; Pierce, Eininger, Allen, and Donnette 1995). Another common approach is to highlight specific programs as models. For instance, Patricia Hynes's *A Patch of Eden* (1996) includes descriptions of successful garden programs in Harlem, San Francisco, Philadelphia, and Chicago. By sharing personal accounts from participants, descriptive books such as these convey the capacity of gardens to serve both individual and community needs, be it a geographical neighborhood or a need- or interest-based group. Such sources provide a glimpse into a community garden at a particular moment in its evolution. However, while showcasing a successful garden helps to catalyze interest in community gardens, the evolving nature of most community gardens requires open-ended, situational description.

1.7

This gardener has been part of the Ocean View Farms in West Los Angeles for many years. Resting for a moment, he gladly shares his memories of his childhood victory garden. Photograph by Lewis Watts, 2001.

Research on Benefits Associated with Community Gardens

Given the multiple benefits associated with community gardens, it is not surprising that researchers have turned to the gardens and their participants to study a range of social, individual, and community processes. Environmental psychologists, historians, horticulturists, geographers, leisure studies experts, and others have conducted qualitative and quantitative research that either directly studies aspects of community gardens or has inferred associations with them.

As illustrated in descriptive accounts of participants, community gardens provide individuals with many important personal benefits, including psychological restoration, connection to nature, cultural expression, self-esteem, and personal growth. While very subjective, the consistency in self-reports merits study into how gardening fosters these outcomes. Research by environmental psychologists Rachel and Stephen Kaplan has been instrumental in describing the ability of gardening and viewing green spaces to provide psychological restoration, in the context of both backyard and community gardening (Kaplan 1973, 1983). For example, one study found that gardening satisfied people through tangible results, personal involvement in cultivation, and sustained interest in gardening as relaxation, diversion, and a hobby (Kaplan 1973). Horticulturist Diane Relf (1979) and Charles Lewis (1979) describe therapeutic opportunities associated with community gardening. Charles Lewis, horticulturist at Morton Arboretum and past juror for the New York City Housing Authority tenant garden contest, noted that people appreciate plants because they reveal enduring patterns in life, are nonjudgmental, and respond to care by growing. Based on his experience and drawing on horticultural therapy, Charles Lewis's *Green Nature/Human Nature* (1996) considers gardens as restorative environments for stressful urban lifestyles and social isolation.

In addition to studies that analyze the personal benefits associated with gardening, there also are studies that address the social benefits of participation in collective gardening. Community gardens provide clues to social processes in motion and provide physical manifestations of urban activism and cultural expression. Historical accounts by Thomas Bassett (1981), Sam Bass Warner (1987), Brian Trelstad (1997), Laura Lawson (2005), and others have looked to past phases of garden promotion to understand how participation in gardening satisfied social concerns of past phases of community gardening activity. Others have focused on current community gardens to illustrate cultural expression and neighborhood or city politics associated with gardens as claimed space. For example, in her research on community gardens in the Lower East Side of New York, geographer Karen Schmelzkopf (1995) outlines how participants claimed unused space to serve varied needs yet faced conflict with development pressures for housing and community gentrification. Others have considered community gardens as artifacts that display cultural traditions and adaptations by immigrant groups, such as documentation on the casita gardens in New York, Philadelphia, and elsewhere (Aponte-Pares 1996; Winterbottom 1998). Leisure studies scholar Troy Glover (2003) has conducted several studies that analyze the meaning gardens hold for participants, including as symbols of collective resistance, production of social capital, and support of democratic values (Glover 2003; Glover 2004; Glover, Shinew, and Parry 2005). Sociologist Michael Jamison (1985) uses the community garden movement to illustrate conflicting interpretations of meaning and organization between dominant bureaucratic structures and social movement organizations.

This body of research continues to grow and is grounded in a range of disciplines. Unfortunately, disciplinary boundaries tend to isolate research efforts. To

1.8
During the 1994 American Community Gardening Conference in Chicago, Slumbusters founders Gerald and Lorean Earles gave a tour of one of their gardens and showed an award they received from the President George Bush's Points of Light program in support of volunteerism. Photograph by Laura Lawson, 1994.

date, there is no clearinghouse or easily referenced source that bridges the literature or provides information on recent publications about research related to community gardens.

Community Gardens as Discussed in Planning and Design Literature

In general, community gardening has been a relatively small part of planning and design literature. When community gardening is discussed, it is generally in the context of illustrating community open space, community revitalization, urban ecology, or community food security. Most considerations of community gardening in design and planning assume the psychological and social benefits that are outlined through descriptive accounts and research, and focus primarily on how participation results in new community resources and spaces.

When the concept of community open space emerged in the 1980s, community gardens were one of the most commonly cited examples of alternatives to parks and plazas. One of the first studies of community open space involved an interdisciplinary team from landscape architecture, environmental psychology, urban design, and architecture in a multimethod inventory of 410 community-built spaces in New York City, of which 69 percent included vegetable gardening as a land use. This research project helped catalyze the Neighborhood Open Space Coalition, and results were published in two books: *Community Open Spaces: Greening Neighbor-hoods through Community Action and Land Conservation* (Francis, Cashdan, and Paxson 1984) and *Struggle for Space: The Greening of New York City, 1970–1984* (Fox, Koeppel, and Kellam 1985). Landscape architect Mark Francis has continued to be a pivotal supporter of community gardens and has published ongoing research on the social dynamics of community gardens as open space. In one study that compared a community garden to an adjacent park, Francis (1987) uncovered perceptual differences held by users, park officials, and neighbors that suggested public appreciation of the community gardens as cared-for spaces that facilitated particular recreational and social needs.

Community gardens are also referenced as a catalyst for community partici-pation and community revitalization. Designers are attracted to the concept of individuals in a community getting together to take over a vacant lot or unkempt school ground and creating gardens. Karl Linn (1991) described community gar-dens as a kind of urban barn raising that brought community members together on a shared project. Landscape architect Randy Hester has been a long-standing advocate of community gardens as both places of participation and ecological grounding (Hester 1984). Community gardens are interwoven into Hester's *Design for Ecological Democracy* (2007) as illustrations of community commons, places of learning, and multicultural gatherings. Citing model programs and successes, designers and planners encourage the idea to go forward in other communities. For instance, in *Old Cities/Green Cities* (2002), written by Blaine Bonham, Gerri Spilka, and Darl Rastorfer and published by the American Planning Association, a strategy to address urban vacant land includes community gardening and greening along with development of lower-density housing and open space, "green industries," and other strategies, citing model programs in Philadelphia and elsewhere.

Recently, urban planning discourse has increased attention to issues of food access and systems at the state and local level. As argued by Kameshwari Pothuku-chi and Jerome Kaufman (2000), local food networks are an important planning concern because not only is food access a basic human need but food systems can also be included as an essential part of the local economy, public health, and natu-ral environment. Community food security is defined as "a situation in which all community residents obtain a safe, culturally acceptable, nutritionally adequate diet through a sustainable food system that maximizes community self-reliance and social justice" (Hamm and Bellows 2003, 37). Along with other measures, including farmers' markets, local food industries, grocery store cooperatives, and school gar-dens, community gardens increase options for individuals to acquire food locally.

Community gardens are often included in ecological visions of residential communities and urban development. In the design of planned communities, the desire to address basic household needs—including food access—within the home environment or neighborhood has been a recurring theme, from company towns like the 1919 Billerica Garden Suburb in Massachusetts to federal efforts in community planning, such as the New Deal community of Greenbelt, Maryland. Such proposals often include community gardens and allotments close to homes so that residents can grow their own food. Village Homes in Davis, California, is an oft-cited example of an ecologically designed community, and community gardens and communal agriculture figure into its design and social opportunities (Corbett and Corbett 2000; Francis 2003). Community gardens also contribute to the ecological ideal by allowing people to acquire their basic needs locally, reduce the transportation costs of food, and reconnect to environmental processes and food production (Hough 1984; Spirn 1984). Gardening is conceptually and practically linked to other ecological processes, such as composting, reducing waste, active living, addressing the urban heat-island effect, and creating habitat.

In a more philosophical approach, landscape architect Anne Whiston Spirn's *Language of Landscape* (1998) illustrates the connection that people have with their environment through sharing stories from her work with community garden groups in Philadelphia. She describes the "messy vitality" of community gardens as expressions of the people and their ongoing connection with the sites and their processes.

ROLES AND RESOURCES COMMUNITY GARDENS PROVIDE

As the literature indicates, community gardens are cited as resources that provide an array of potential benefits. Most participants consider community gardening a way to achieve multiple and integrated social, personal, and environmental goals, including connection with nature, physical exercise, health and nutrition, self-esteem, environmental education, personal growth, companionship, skill development, cultural expression, income generation, empowerment, and more. Some of the attributed benefits are very tangible, such as growing food and creating new open space, while others are intangible, such as the psychological benefits or appreciating ecological processes. Still others require time and other factors to be realized, such as the empowerment that can result from ongoing efforts to improve a community.

While participants may have personal experiences that validate these expectations, it is sometimes difficult to extrapolate to other people and situations. Garden promoters often credit community gardens as a way to achieve multiple benefits, yet convincing skeptical nonparticipants may be hindered by overly general and often unproven claims. Gardens may garner general support through their assumed goodness, but without clarifying how and why gardens serve the public, they can fall victim to "higher and better uses" as determined by social norms and policies (Jamison 1985).

To aid planners, designers, and policy makers in identifying beneficial outcomes possible through community gardens, we need to look at the unique characteristics of community gardens that distinguish them from parks and other forms of open space and that facilitate their ability to serve different needs. As Mark Francis (1987) noted in his comparison of an adjacent park and community garden, strong conceptual differences exist between types of open space. These qualities have to do with open spaces as places for people to garden, provision of space for gardening, the community aspect of shared gardens, educational and training programs at gardens, and urban sustainability.

Places for People to Garden

It is appropriate to consider how the community garden is both a place—a garden—and an opportunity to act—to garden (Francis and Hester 1990). Through access to land and the act of participating, individuals and groups access an array of resources, including food, environmental restoration, and personal expression.

At its most basic level, the community garden provides a place for people to grow vegetables, fruit, and herbs for consumption. Various studies have documented harvest returns, with results varying according to climate, context, and other factors. For example, a 1987 survey of the Philadelphia Urban Garden Program found that community garden plots yielded $160 worth of produce for an average investment of $47, and that gardeners ate significantly more vegetables than nongardeners (Blair, Giesecke, and Sherman 1991). A 1989 study in Newark found that an average 720-square-foot plot earned $500 from a $25 investment (Patel 1991). In addition to growing food to subsidize household expenses, gardening provides an opportunity to grow foods that may be difficult or expensive to acquire otherwise. It is quite common to see food grown that reflects ethnic or cultural heritage, such as Latino farmers in Los Angeles growing nopales or Asian American gardeners in Seattle growing bok choy. In cases of entrepreneurial or job-training gardens, trainees or employees grow food to sell locally, such as the Food Project in Lincoln, Massachusetts, or the Homeless Garden Project in Santa Cruz, California.

The community garden also provides a place to grow plants for reasons other than human consumption. Often described as "urban nature," "natural oases," or "slices of nature," community gardens represent the opportunity to personally engage with natural systems. The community garden becomes a place to illustrate new ideas about urban ecology and conservation. Many gardens promote organic practices, composting, and seed saving. Quite often, gardens include areas devoted to native plants, butterfly gar-

1.9
Family showing their harvest from their plot at the Ocean View Farms in West Los Angeles. Photograph by Lewis Watts, 2001.

dens, and drought-tolerant plants. These areas may serve as "demonstration sites" intended to inspire and educate visitors. Community gardens can become sites to model sustainable storm water catchment systems, creative reuse of materials, or new sustainable materials and technologies.

Whether involved in growing food, tending flowers, or stewarding habitats, participants enjoy the community garden as a place to garden. Many people consider gardening to be an important source of leisure, both in terms of physical recreation and emotional restoration. To many participants, the community garden provides respite from urban stressors of noise, crowds, traffic, and the predominance of paved surfaces. Very subjective benefits—the ability to simply view plants and the act of gardening to sooth tensions inherent in urban living—have found some validity in research conducted by environmental psychologists Rachel Kaplan (1973, 1983) and Roger Ulrich (1984). Health-related research has supported the importance of gardening for the well-being of individuals, particularly through development of social and individual skills and the enjoyment of leisure and natural surroundings (Smith 1998, Moore 1989). The therapeutic benefits of gardens have been the focus of a growing design as well as health-care related literature (Cooper Marcus and Barnes 1999; Ulrich 1999).

The Community Aspect of Community Gardens

The key aspect of community gardens that distinguish them from traditional parks is that participants tend the garden and shape its evolution. Planting, cultivation, harvest, and overall maintenance are all the responsibility of participants. As a shared resource—a commons—the garden must be negotiated so that people understand the expectations and requirements necessary for its sustainability. Gardens bring people together who might not otherwise interact.

As neighbors collectively work to establish a garden out of nothing, they develop social networks and learn organizing skills. The capacity to support community dialogue is essential, as garden participation evolves and communities change. In some cases, this organization has saved gardens from demolition. In other cases, success in community gardening has led to other local campaigns, such as street cleanups or efforts in community economic development.

In addition to the gardeners who literally have their hands in the dirt to sustain the garden, community gardens also may engage other groups who provide technical, financial, or moral support. For instance, community gardens frequently enjoy collaboration with volunteers who have gone through the cooperative extension Master Gardener program that teaches individuals about gardening and in return requires a certain number of volunteer hours for community outreach. Sometimes school groups, service groups, and others participate in a garden's special workday or event. In addition to direct participation, many others may be engaged through their membership in citywide organizations with missions to promote and sus-

1.10
The Village Homes
community in Davis,
California, is a model
of ecological- and
community-sensitive
design and includes a
community garden as well
as communal orchards and
vineyards. Photo courtesy
of Judy Corbett.

1.11
A gardener meeting and
potluck at Wattles Farm
and Neighborhood Garden
in Hollywood, California.
Photograph by Laura
Lawson, 2001.

tain gardens throughout the city, such as New York's Green Guerillas, the Denver
Urban Gardeners (DUG), and Seattle's P-Patch program. Often, cities with several
gardening and greening groups form networks to share resources and outreach
opportunities, such as Chicago's GreenNet and Boston Natural Areas Network.

Education and Training Programs Affiliated with Community Gardens

Community gardening is often considered a way to engage individuals and groups in learning about multiple subjects, including nature, community, and self. Quite often, a community garden will include educational plots or signage to inform participants and passersby of particular activities or processes at work. Many community gardening organizations have child- and adult-education programs to teach gardening, recycling, composting, and nutrition.

The capacity of gardening to teach about nutrition and ecology has led to many efforts to promote gardening in schools. In fact, the school garden has been a recurring effort since the 1890s that is currently enjoying a rebirth, with California leading the way with the "garden in every school" campaign. Many community garden groups work with school programs to promote intergenerational activities and neighborhood outreach. The Garden Mosaics program, developed by the Department of Natural Resources at Cornell, includes an exercise to document a community garden by conducting site observation and interviewing gardeners. The goal is to simultaneously provide scientific learning, intergenerational mentoring, and expanded cultural understanding while building a database on community gardens around the nation.

Another recurring theme in education is related to job training and local entrepreneurial development. Many gardens provide these services to at-risk teenagers, exconvicts, the homeless, and others. Through the process of caring for the site and growing crops, the participants learn skills that may be transferable to landscaping or nursery work, but more importantly they learn about teamwork and responsibility (Lawson and McNally 1999).

URBAN SUSTAINABILITY AND THE URBAN COMMUNITY GARDEN

Sustainability has been an important topic in urban planning discourse since the late 1980s. Different from other compartmentalized theories and practices of planning, the discourse of sustainability emphasizes the connections among social, economic, and environmental issues while also grappling with solutions to improve conditions for future generations. Because community gardens address a wide range of social, economic, and environmental concerns, they provide a tangible manifestation of the holistic concept of urban sustainability. Community gardens are a resource that individuals and families can use to meet everyday needs while also facilitating active living, self-reliance, and reduction in consumption. As places that bring people together, both literally and conceptually, community gardens facilitate neighborly contact that expands social networks and the sharing of knowledge and skills. The development and characteristics of community gardens rely on local activism and participation, which foster cultural expression and inspire

1.12
The Edible School Yard at Martin Luther King, Jr., Middle School in Berkeley, California, was started in 1994 as the dream of renowned restaurateur Alice Waters of Chez Panisse to provide healthy food for schoolchildren to eat while also making connections between gardening, cooking, and various parts of the school curriculum. Photograph by Laura Lawson, 2001.

efforts toward other aspects of neighborhood revitalization. They create habitat for other species to increase biodiversity in urban areas. And like a natural ecosystem, an urban community garden facilitates these diverse capacities through interdependence so that participation may reap multiple and interconnected benefits.

UNDERSTANDING COMMUNITY GARDENS

While the proposition to provide space for people to garden in cities may seem basic, this overview illustrates the many meanings, resources, and expectations bound within the concept of community gardening. The simultaneous nature of community gardens as physical space, participant-driven effort, and programmed activity all contribute to their ability to serve a wide range of urban concerns, from food access and nutrition to social justice and education. A recurring feature in American cities, the community garden is not only a tangible resource for individuals and communities but also an organizing concept for new ideas about quality of life and urban sustainability. This overview helps to explain why garden participants and advocates have so much faith that community gardening can achieve so many beneficial outcomes. As the benefits of community gardens become more widely recognized and better understood, the opportunity to affirm their public capacity through planning and design becomes especially critical. The next step is to understand what is involved in the creation, maintenance, evolution, and sustainability of community gardens.

1.13
While growing and selling organic produce, youth employed at the Berkeley Youth Alternative's Community Garden Patch also learn valuable job skills such as teamwork, accountability, marketing, and sales. Photograph by Laura Lawson, 1995.

2

Making and Sustaining a Community Garden

Community gardens require a different perspective on design and planning than is traditionally understood for public open space. As part of the open-space system, community gardens serve many public functions yet are distinct from traditional parks because they are maintained by the participants and they evolve according to community participation and interest. Community gardens maintain an ambiguous position as both public and private forms: serving an array of recreational, social, and environmental benefits while being shaped and maintained by participants who often also benefit personally as well. The challenge for planners, designers, and policy makers is to consider how gardens serve active participants and the larger community while also acknowledging unique considerations that distinguish such gardens from other types of public space. To aid in this understanding, this chapter outlines specific issues relevant to the making and sustaining of community gardens. In particular, the chapter will address aspects of garden creation, site considerations, planning processes, participation, maintenance and implementation, evaluation, and city planning perspectives. This general discussion provides some background for understanding both the consistent patterns and the uniqueness of the case studies that follow.

INITIAL CONCEPTION

Community gardens arise out of a demand that manifests itself in activism. Most community gardens are started by individuals who realize a need or desire for gardening and either make that need known to a public agency or institution, or take matters into their own hands to acquire a site and create a community garden. These individuals may be neighbors seeking to garden in their community or members of a school or institution who consider gardening as a means to facilitate related objectives, such as environmental education or community outreach. Sometimes the community garden addresses the need of a particular immigrant group to retain cultural traditions and provide economic opportunity. Whatever the reason, rarely is a garden already available and prepared for their use. Instead, individuals and groups must take the initiative to organize and develop a strategy to create a garden.

In most cases, success relies on developing relationships and collaborating with other groups. At this point in the evolution of the community gardening movement, most city governments have some experience with community gardening, and many have policies or offices that support or at least oversee community-based efforts to start new gardens; often it is the parks and recreation department, a neighborhood council, or social service agency. There may be a citywide organization—either a city or nonprofit agency —with experience in starting community gardens. Or support may come from a cooperative extension, a local college or university, a local environmental organization, or a coalition representing all of these groups. Partnerships help sustain projects by blending gardener participation with technical assistance, volunteer networks, in-kind donations, programmatic support, and funding. Each locale has a different approach that is shaped by local traditions of activism, willingness to collaborate, and dedicated resources.

THE GARDEN SITE

In most cases, community gardens are located on land that would otherwise be underutilized—previously vacant lots, transportation rights-of-way, little-used sections of a park, or other undeveloped land. Often, people who are interested in starting a garden conduct an inventory of the community to identify potential sites and then begin the process of getting permission to use the land, either from a public or private party. In the hopes of success, many groups seek to make the most of otherwise problematic situations or collaborative opportunities, such as seeking to use a site that is too steep for housing, or lobbying for inclusion in a new park or housing development.

Mechanisms for securing access to land include squatting, leasing, inclusion in a public recreation area, and ownership by the gardening group, supporting nonprofit, or land trust. The local economic and political climate has an impact on the procedure for land acquisition, terms of use, and assurance of permanence. Historically, many community gardens were temporary uses of land during times of low development pressure, and with each phase of garden promotion, new land had to be acquired (Lawson 2005). In some cases, gardens started as World War II victory

2.1
In 1993, the idea to start the Berkeley Youth Alternative's garden on this bare site was daunting, considering the lack of organic matter and compacted soils on this former railroad corridor. It was leased from the city on a three-year renewable contract with provision that no permanent structures be built. Photograph by Laura Lawson, 1993.

2.2
Three years after its groundbreaking, the Berkeley Youth Alternative's Community Garden Patch is a lush site that includes community garden plots, a youth market garden, and a children's garden. Photograph by Laura Lawson, 1996.

gardens have continued to be cultivated, evolving into community gardens that still exist today, such as in Washington D. C., Boston, Chicago, and elsewhere. While many groups that organize a community garden may use temporary land-acquisition procedures, they generally intend their garden to be permanent.

In communities that have experienced vast disinvestment, activists may just start gardening on a site with no resistance or attention from city agencies or absentee land owners. Some city administrations are very supportive and have established procedures to promote community gardens on public land. Other cities have policies that allow for community gardens on a temporary basis that must give way to "higher and better use" if the land is needed for something else. Sometimes the leadership in a particular public agency paves the way by encouraging community gardens, such as a utility company that wants residents to use land under power lines or a parks agency that engages the community in park planning. In other cases, an agency may put up resistance, citing the unkempt appearance of a community garden or concerns about liability.

The most common type of site procurement is the short-term lease. Gardeners typically arrange with public or private landowners to donate or rent land at nominal rates, often with the agreement that the gardeners will leave the site in good condition upon the owner's request. While this arrangement is usually the quickest and least controversial way to gain access, it has drawbacks in terms of longevity. For neighbors who are eager to start gardening, a lease arrangement of one dollar per year sounds very appealing. For the owner—the city, an institution, or an individual—such an arrangement allows the site to be used and maintained by others without jeopardizing the possibility of later development. The aura of permanence that established fruit trees and richly cultivated soil give to a ten-year-old garden may belie the vulnerability of an annually renewed lease. Leasing public land is no more secure than leasing private land, as these sites are just as likely to be developed for other public purposes or sold if development pressure makes that land valuable in times of tight public budgets. In some cities, long-term leases at slightly higher rental rates have been established.

Another approach is to integrate community gardens into the public recreation system, either on undeveloped park property or within existing parks. In the former case, a parks district may acquire land in response to a demand for community gardening or may allow community gardening on an underutilized site or one that later will be redeveloped into another form of recreation. In the case of community gardens being put into larger parks, the garden becomes one more recreational activity, along with playgrounds, sports fields, and dog runs. Occasionally, an official or local resident may raise concerns about the appropriateness of gardens within parks, sometimes alluding to the individual "ownership" of plots to serve personal food needs. Garden advocates counter this argument by both citing the public functions community gardens serve and comparing gardening to other publicly provided recreational facilities that have limited general public use/appeal, such as golf ranges and tennis courts. Advocates can assuage such concerns by committing to broad public involvement through educational programs, workshops, tours, and special events.

The ultimate form of site security is to own the site through the purchase by a community group, a supportive nonprofit organization, or a land trust. According to an American Community Gardening Association (ACGA) survey in 1996,

5.3 percent of community gardens in thirty-eight cities were in land trust or on land owned by the gardening organization. While ownership is clearly a winning solution to assure long-term gardening, as a sustainability strategy it may overlook environmental justice implications—while wealthy neighborhoods may have the resources and connections to buy their garden sites, poorer neighborhoods, even organized ones, may not have the necessary resources or social connections. In recent years, a preferred strategy is the creation of a neighborhood land trust to purchase garden sites or negotiate conservation easements of private land (Schukoske 2000). Land trusts may reflect a larger trend toward public/private partnerships that are taking an increasingly prominent role in the upkeep of parks and public space in America (Project for Public Spaces 2000). Usually land trusts establish procedures that ensure that the community gardening group is well organized and attend to ongoing participation and site maintenance. The typical trust agrees to hold the deed, ensure that property taxes are paid or exempt, provide liability insurance, and serve as a communication and reference tool to facilitate operations. In return, the garden group typically establishes a management structure and agrees to abide by guidelines that address site security, maintenance and group communication requirements, public access, and other elements.

2.3
Located along one edge of the Fens in Boston, the Fenway Community Garden includes public pathways through the plots, allowing passersby to see what the gardeners are doing. Photograph by Vanessa Lee, 2007.

DESIGN AND DESIGN PROCESS

A community garden's design varies with its context and participants. Quite often the design unfolds through incremental development of a site, with decisions about the locations of gardening plots, paths, and common areas determined by the participants who are constructing and using the site. In other cases, a master plan is developed to guide site development that may occur all at once or through phases. Almost always, the founding gardeners are involved in the initial site design, which evolves based on the needs, ideas, and inspirations of later gardeners. Often, the gardeners receive design assistance from city parks staff and/or professional designers who are either hired or offer services pro bono (Johnson 2005).

While the design of garden sites is as varied as the communities in which they are located, there are some basic considerations that gardeners share. A fundamental concern is the ability of plants to flourish through attention to hours of sunlight, tillable soil, water, and access to amendments. Given that many gardens are established on previously damaged or difficult sites, often the first step is to evaluate the soil quality and develop a strategy to improve the soil through composting, mulching, and amendments. Lead in the soil may be an issue, requiring considerations of imported dirt and limited areas for edible plants (Cohen 1986).

The framework for the garden itself is often determined by participants' ideas about how to allocate land for individual plots, paths, and common areas. The size and configuration of garden plots vary with the site and community. One garden may have five-by-ten-feet wood-sided raised beds, while another may have in-ground plots of twenty-by-twenty feet or larger. Many gardens have accessible beds that are raised to allow persons in wheelchairs to garden. Typically, a garden plot is allocated to an individual or household, although many gardens also have communal or shared plots where gardeners can share herbs or other special crops or where they can help grow food for food banks. Plots may be allotted to individuals or organized into "pods" to ease governance and encourage social interaction of smaller groups.

The design of the perimeter area is of critical importance for both security and public appearance. The general feeling is that appearance does affect public perception of the garden and that neat and attractive edges promote community support. Many gardens include ornamental plantings, flowers, and herbs in beds along street frontage, not only to provide an aesthetically pleasing view for passersby but also to create areas where it is

2.4
Youth work with a landscape architecture graduate student to develop the children's garden area at the Berkeley Youth Alternative's Community Garden Patch. Photograph by Laura Lawson, 1995.

2.5
A group of youth from the San Francisco League of Urban Gardeners work with residents of the Kuhio Park Terrace public housing project in Honolulu, Hawaii, to build a raised bed for a new community garden. Photograph by Laura Lawson, 1998.

acceptable for passersby to pick and sample what is within their reach. While most gardeners acknowledge that there is some pilfering, if not outright vandalism, their approaches to addressing this concern range from acceptance of the loss as part of the urban context to encouraging the potential culprits to be legitimate participants, by securing the site through fences and locked gates. Some garden groups report that low fences of three to four feet reinforce territoriality and provide sufficient security, while others have felt compelled to build taller fences.

Most community gardens also have common areas and gathering spaces that serve practical and social needs. A lawn area, patio, casita, or other shared space provides a site for group meetings, a notice board, picnic tables, barbeque grills, and so on. Many gardens include shared toolsheds, compost bins, and waste piles, while some also have beehives, communal orchards and herb gardens, children's play areas, or other features. Because most gardens need occasional deliveries of mulch and compost, another design consideration is provision of a delivery area that is accessible to trucks and linked to the garden's path system so that gardeners can wheelbarrow the materials to other areas in the garden.

While gardens share some basic components, the resulting designs vary according to local conditions and community interests. Some gardens are designed for

2.6
At Woodcliff Community Garden in Boston, staff from the Boston Urban Gardeners designed this raised bed to make it easier for elderly individuals to garden. A bench at the end provides a place to store materials. Photograph by Laura Lawson, 1992.

2.7
At the Gilbert Street Garden in Durham, North Carolina, organized by the South Eastern Efforts Developing Sustainable Spaces (SEEDS), local artist Mark Elliott contributed an inviting gate made of welded steel. Photograph by Laura Lawson, 1999.

efficiency, providing plots of uniform size, with narrow walkways between plots and a wider pathway through the garden, usually with a central waterline and water spigots along the path. Other gardens are designed as artistic expressions, with sculpture and shaped beds—such as butterflies or peace signs. Anne Whiston Spirn (1998) considers the design of a garden to reflect the garden community's process— a garden designed for efficient allotment suggests many minds and bodies working together but individually, while a more amorphously designed garden reflects one shared concept.

2.8
At the Watts Growing Project in Los Angeles, this fencing made from jean belting material suggests access to materials from the nearby garment district. Photograph by Laura Lawson, 1998.

IMPLEMENTATION AND MAINTENANCE

Rarely is a community garden design realized in one phase; instead, most gardens evolve and require many growing seasons to be implemented. The garden's design must be amenable to change over time as the community changes. Most implementation efforts rely on volunteer workdays and special events that bring participants and others together to accomplish tasks. Landscape architect Karl Linn described this process as a contemporary barn-raising activity that brings neighbors together for a shared resource (Linn 1991, 1999). Making such workdays into social events that include food, music, and other pleasurable activities encourages participation and helps to build stronger community support.

Most garden groups develop rules to aid in the garden's development and upkeep. Typically, gardeners agree to maintain their plot and the paths surrounding it, to avoid shading or causing harm to neighboring plots, and to participate in overall garden maintenance activities. Often, they agree to be on a subcommittee, such as a group that oversees the compost area or produces a quarterly newsletter. Many gardens have policies that prohibit planting woody plants in individual plots, since these can cause shade and become a problem later if the garden plot transfers hands. Instead, fruiting trees and other woody plants are often provided in common areas or along the garden periphery. Some gardens require that all plants be produced organically, without pesticides or herbicides. Others do not have such restrictions.

Given that there is no one way to garden, the gardening group must also negotiate cultural differences and approaches to gardening. While one gardener may plant in rows and diligently remove all weeds from his or her plot and path, another

2.9
Mailboxes along a path at the Ocean View Farms in West Los Angeles provide a way for gardeners to communicate. Photograph by Laura Lawson, 2001.

2.10
The Clinton Community Garden in New York City includes a park-like area at its center, with individual garden plots located along the periphery. Photograph by Laura Lawson, 1992.

gardener may plant in a more random style and allow plants to reseed. Immigrants from agrarian backgrounds may seek to maximize their gardening area or garden in a vertical system that casts shadows on other plots. These are issues that must be addressed by the group.

PARTICIPATION AND LEADERSHIP

Whereas a tennis court can go underutilized for months without significant impact on its ability to be used in the future, a community garden requires constant care and upkeep. Gardens are volunteer efforts, and the commitment required to maintain them—from the cultivation of a plot to being part of the governance—is essential to the garden's sustainability. The degree of participation varies. Some gardens are spearheaded by a strong charismatic leader or core group of individuals who set the process in motion and take responsibility for most of the garden's collective needs, including compost delivery, collecting garden plot fees, assigning new gardeners, and maintaining insurance. In fortunate cases, the volunteer leaders realize enough personal satisfaction to continue; however, sometimes these individuals burn out or move, leaving a gap in leadership. Some participants simply want a place to garden and do not get involved in garden organization or politics. Just like any group activity, interpersonal dynamics influence garden functioning. Some gardens may have clear rules that make involvement easy, while others may struggle with opposing ideas about how to garden and share responsibility. Gardens in high demand may have waiting lists and procedures for quick reallocation, while others may go through periods of underutilization and may struggle with overall site maintenance.

Because community gardens are built and maintained by their users, they are often considered models for community participation and empowerment. However, this is not an inherent condition, and the demands involved in sustaining participation should not be overlooked. Past manifestations, particularly those associated with education and income subsidies, were often run in a top-down manner that minimized the decision-making role of participants (Lawson 2005). Enthusiasm for community gardens during the 1970s sometimes led city agencies to develop gardens without assuring local interest, resulting in underutilized and neglected spaces. Today, most community garden advocates stress development of leadership and participatory processes as much, if not more, than site development techniques. Because public support is necessary to acquire land, fund programs, and increase community involvement, many garden organizations have developed policies to promote outreach and community involvement. Regular open-gate hours, events, educational programs, and collaborations with local institutions such as churches and schools are examples of such outreach. The ACGA is also increasing its lobbying efforts at the local, state, and national level.

Some groups stay informal, working in an isolated garden or under the oversight of a citywide gardening organization. Others form into nonprofit organizations in order to qualify for grants and acquire liability protection, and therefore must comply with state laws about annual meetings, elections, bylaws, and other considerations. No matter how autonomous a garden group seems, it often needs outside resources, ranging from basic materials, such as mulch from the city's waste department, to more complicated resources, such as getting water at agricultural rather than urban rates. Staffed organizations—either city agencies or nonprofit organizations—often help make these resources available. Many of these organizations are staffed by individuals with educational or career backgrounds in horticulture, community development, education, landscape architecture, or other fields. These staff members typically work closely with garden leaders and often arrange citywide meetings to encourage dialogue between garden groups, city agencies, and other supportive institutions. Such groups include New York's Green Guerillas, the Denver Urban Gardeners (DUG), Durham's South Eastern Efforts Developing Sustainable Spaces (SEEDS), and others.

EVOLUTION AND EVALUATION

Just as the plants and conditions of the garden site change with time, so too does the community that uses the garden. A neighborhood may change in terms of income, race, ethnicity, language, age, or other factors. For this reason, constant reflection and evaluation are important considerations to assure garden sustainability. A garden may have an efficient system of site allocation and maintenance yet still require semiregular meetings to check if new issues are emerging that need to be addressed.

The need for evaluation is particularly critical for community gardens that provide environmental education or other services. It becomes imperative to document results to demonstrate success to funders and supporters. At the same time, programmatic needs may shift. For example, a program with a K–6 gardening element may find that it needs to expand to junior high or high school youth, or vice versa. A program with environmental education may find that local drought conditions create a new demand for demonstration areas that show drought-tolerant plants and landscape strategies. New partners can join the effort as priorities and programs change.

CITYWIDE PLANNING

While each garden may develop its own idiosyncratic character, a citywide view suggests another way to evaluate service and assure sustainability. When considered individually, a single garden may not seem significant to the overall city planning strategy, but a comprehensive evaluation may show a system of gardens that serve as community resources with the potential to serve the larger public open-space network. Similarly, it may not be alarming to see that a particular garden is on a site zoned for housing, but if an analysis shows that many community gardens in a city or neighborhood are vulnerable to "higher and better use" because of their zoning designation, it may become essential to address community gardening as part of the city-planning process.

In order to understand the larger context that is influencing community garden sustainability, many groups have undertaken citywide inventories and mapping projects. In 1996, Boston Futures (now Boston Natural Areas Network) developed an inventory guide to analyze the capital and maintenance needs of sixty gardens owned by nonprofit organizations. More recently there have been efforts to create interactive mapping exercises that are available to the public on the Web. The New York City Community Gardening Mapping Project is an interactive Web site that locates gardens within their neighborhood context and provides information about zoning, ownership, garden provisions, and events. The Department of Natural Resources at Cornell University has developed the Garden Mosaics program that not only provides educational curricula for youth but also contributes to an online database on community gardens that the ACGA supports. These mapping and inventory projects help to reveal the breadth and scope of gardening efforts underway in one city. This becomes an important advocacy tool to show the collective interest in gardening. It can also show vulnerabilities, such as gardens on sites zoned for other uses or areas of the city that are underserved. Such insights are needed to more effectively articulate the values, roles, and models of community gardens to better secure them as legitimate and protected city open spaces.

There are interesting approaches being implemented in various cities. In Berkeley, California, for example, the general plan supports community gardens by promoting public purchase of land, providing long-term leases, encouraging partnerships, and providing in-kind contributions and resources. Community gardens have a specific zoning category in Boston and Portland that protects them as public open space. In Chicago, the city created NeighborSpace as a nonprofit land trust, with representatives from city agencies on its boards and agreements about procedures for public land acquisition in place. Strategies to facilitate community garden sustainability are constantly evolving.

2.11
Gardens become sites of expression for individuals and show the solidarity of a group. At the South Central Farm in Los Angeles, one gardener included an altar in his plot. Photograph by Lewis Watts, 2001.

2.12
Murals enliven the bare walls surrounding this garden run by the Village of the Arts and Humanities in Philadelphia. Photograph by Laura Lawson, 1999.

3

Seattle Model

LOCAL ACTIVISM AND INSTITUTIONAL SUPPORT

Community gardens have been a visible feature in Seattle's urban landscape since the 1970s. They can be found in the city's downtown core and in its suburbs, in residential zones and industrial areas, in rich and poor neighborhoods, and in marginal areas as well as established urban parks. The widespread presence of community gardens is a result of a combination of factors ranging from a favorable climate to popular interest in gardening to institutional support. This chapter takes a broad perspective on how a network of actors and resources contribute to the creation and continuation of community gardens throughout the city. It serves as a context for the garden case studies in part 2.

GEOGRAPHY AND LOCAL ECONOMY

Geographically, Seattle enjoys an ideal context to support community gardens. Its maritime climate is mild, with cool, wet winters and moderate summers that enable nearly year-round gardening. Puget Sound's flora is indebted to this climate as well as to its topographic variety and ribbons of waterways that flow from the Cascade Mountains to Puget Sound and lowland alluvial soils (Kruckeberg 2003). These conditions once provided for a thriving truck-farming economy, with over 3,000 farmers raising bountiful produce for city residents in the early twentieth century (Crowley 1999) . As the city has expanded, these former agricultural lands have been developed for industrial, residential, and other uses, yet some of these lands have

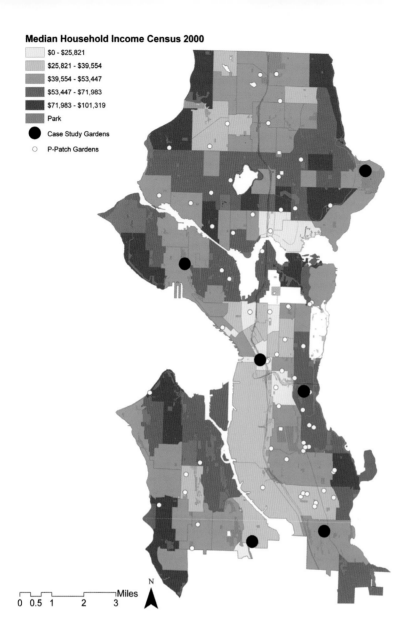

Median Household Income Census 2000

- $0 - $25,821
- $25,821 - $39,554
- $39,554 - $53,447
- $53,447 - $71,983
- $71,983 - $101,319
- Park
- ● Case Study Gardens
- ○ P-Patch Gardens

Miles
0 0.5 1   2   3

N

3.1
Map of household income
in Seattle. Map by Danielle
Pierce and Nathan
Brightbill, with data from
City of Seattle.

been retained or reclaimed for community gardens through the civic activism for which Seattle is well known. The history of Seattle's development and change provides a valuable context for the establishment and support of its diverse community gardens.

With its natural harbor, once-abundant forests, and moderate climate, the Seattle area has long been a gracious home to varied peoples, from the indigenous Native American tribes to its current influx of immigrants. Named after the Suquamish and Duwamish peoples' leader, Chief Seattle, who welcomed the first white settlers who arrived in 1851, the City of Seattle was incorporated in 1869 (Watson 2003; Anderson and Green 2001; Kueter 2001). Since then, it has experienced waves of development and population growth. In 1882 the first steamship left Seattle to cross the Pacific (Kueter 2001). The 1890s brought the arrival of the transcontinental rail line and the Klondike Gold Rush in Alaska, and Seattle flourished as people came to pursue adventure or build businesses to profit from the influx (Kueter 2001).

Seattle and the Puget Sound region have also served as a strategic location for military defense, including Fort Lawton, established in 1900; Sand Point Naval Air Base, started in 1920; and other military installations (Kueter 2001). During World War II, the expansion of shipyards and the aircraft industry helped Seattle emerge from the Great Depression. Seattle's harbor continues to play an important role in its economy, with Seattle identified as one of the nation's top ten container ports, and it provides facilities for cruise ships supporting tourism (Seattle Office of Intergovernmental Relations 2006). Other parts of Seattle's waterfront serve commercial fishing and boating industries.

Today, the Seattle region's economy thrives from a diverse mix that includes "aerospace, information technology, life sciences/biotechnology, clean technology/environmental industries, logistics, and international trade." One of the major employers in the Seattle area is the Boeing Company, which produces commercial airplanes and defense systems. The area is renowned for software jobs and also has over 130 biotechnology firms. Technology and the arts are further advanced through the contributions of multiple public and private universities and colleges in the region (Seattle Office of Intergovernmental Relations 2006).

DEMOGRAPHIC CHANGE

In 2000, 70 percent of Seattle's population was white, reflecting an increase in its minority population from under 6 percent fifty years earlier (Eskenazi 2001; Seattle Office of Intergovernmental Relations 2006). The largest minority group is Asian, comprising approximately 13 percent of the population and including, in descending order of population, Chinese, Filipino, Vietnamese, other Asian ethnicities, Japanese, Korean, and Asian Indian (Seattle Office of Intergovernmental Relations 2006). According to the 2000 U.S. census, which included the option of identifying with one or more races, 9.9 percent of the city's population is African American—alone or in combination with one or more other races—and 5.3 percent is Hispanic/Latino. The city continues to grow in overall population, with an estimated 2005 population of 573,000 within the city, and nearly 3.5 million in the Greater Seattle Area (Seattle Office of Intergovernmental Relations 2006).

While Seattle has many advantages that anchor existing residents and attract new residents to the area, it also has concerns about the phenomena of gentrification and increasing income disparity between the rich and poor. Although the proportion of Seattle residents living in poverty dropped between 1990 and 2000, the actual number of those living in poverty increased, and for certain racial groups and immigrant populations, poverty is a major concern (Seattle Department of

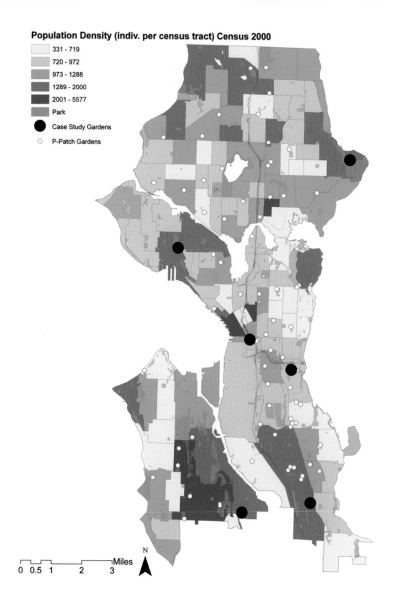

Population Density (indiv. per census tract) Census 2000

- 331 - 719
- 720 - 972
- 973 - 1288
- 1289 - 2000
- 2001 - 5577
- Park
- ● Case Study Gardens
- ○ P-Patch Gardens

Miles
0 0.5 1 2 3

N

3.2
Map of population density
in Seattle. Map by Danielle
Pierce and Nathan
Brightbill, with data from
City of Seattle.

Planning and Development 2003a, 2003b). Among race groups, all nonwhite groups have higher percentages of poverty than whites (8.5 percent), with all but Asians (16.2 percent) more than double the percentage of whites in poverty. While 11 percent of U.S.-born Seattle residents were below the poverty level in 2000, 18 percent of immigrants living in Seattle were below the poverty level, and poverty rates among recent immigrants were higher than immigrants who arrived before 1995 (Seattle Department of Planning and Development 2003b). Between 1990 and 2000, many of Seattle's neighborhoods experienced rapid rises in housing prices. While the dot-com bust in the early 2000s did slow the local economy, housing prices continue to rise. Under the city's recent strategy to encourage growth in the city center, the displacement of existing inner-city communities by new development remains a concern.

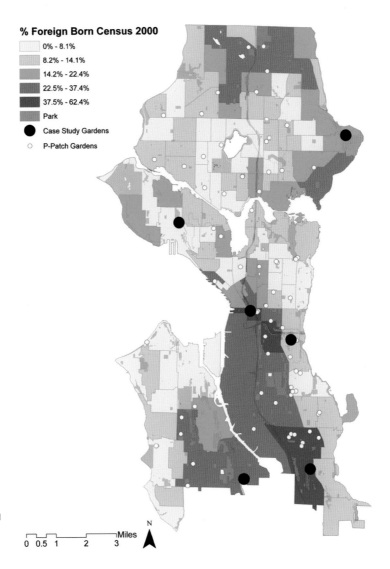

3.3
Map of foreign-born
populations in Seattle.
Map by Danielle Pierce and
Leslie Gia Clark, with data
from City of Seattle.

A CITY OF NEIGHBORHOODS AND CIVIC ACTIVISM

The City of Seattle is organized as a series of neighborhoods that are largely shaped
by the city's topography. Hills, such as Queen Anne Hill, Capitol Hill, and Beacon
Hill, demark neighborhoods, as do valleys, such as Rainier Valley, Madison Valley,
and Interbay. When asked where they live, residents will readily reply with the name
of their neighborhood. This neighborhood focus also is reflected in city politics
and support for locally based initiatives, as well as a strong tradition of civic activism. Activism reaches many levels, from individual to neighborhood to overall city
and region. It can be seen in the development of consumer cooperatives during the
1970s recession, and in various preservation and community-building efforts that
have continued to nurture an informed and active citizenry (PCC Natural Markets
2006). As an example, when the historic Pike Place Market, established in 1907, was

3.4

Federal Emergency Relief Administration Airport Farm, Seattle, September 25, 1934. University Archives, University of Washington Libraries, Special Collections, UW 18910.

threatened by urban renewal in the 1960s, a "Friends of the Market" group formed and successfully lobbied for its protection (Crowley 1999).

Activism also has come from various ethnic groups as an extension of the civil rights movement. In 1970, Native Americans launched a protest to reclaim Seattle's Fort Lawton, based on treaties from 1865 that returned surplus military land to the former owners (McRoberts and Oldham 2003). When most of the site was planned to be decommissioned and the city put forward plans for a large park, Seattle American Indians and supporters protested, organized, and negotiated to ultimately secure land for a cultural center as part of the resulting Discovery Park (Whitebear 1994). Another effort in the 1970s by Latino activists resulted in the development of El Centro de la Raza, "The Center of the People," that provides services to improve people's lives and advance civil rights (Wilma 2000, El Centro de la Raza n.d.). In the predominantly Asian community of the International District, activists fought to protect the historic neighborhood from the construction of a major sports stadium nearby, catalyzing a grassroots movement to revitalize the community. Building on personal friendships and visions of greater justice, activists from differ-ent ethnic communities formed a coalition to support each other (Santos 2002).

Besides civic activism, Seattle also is known for its progressive environmental values, which translate into support for green open space. The city is framed by natural areas, but its neighborhood and community parks, bikeways, and pedes-trian-friendly streets are valued as well. This commitment was evident in the 1968 "Forward Thrust" bond propositions, in which King County voters approved

$118 million for parks and recreation (including an aquarium) among other propositions (McRoberts 1999). In 2000, Seattle voters passed a $198.2 million levy for the city's parks and for recreational uses (Seattle Department of Parks and Recreation 2006). The "Pro Parks" Levy provides support for the acquisition and development of new parks and green open space, including community gardens. It also includes funding for environmental stewardship, maintenance, and programming for seniors and youth (Seattle Department of Parks and Recreation 2007a).

SEATTLE'S COMMUNITY GARDEN HISTORY

Seattle's community gardening tradition extends throughout the twentieth century. Similar to national trends, Seattle has experienced waves of urban gardening interest that have resulted in a range of garden programs. For instance, residents participated in the national gardening campaign of World War I. During the Great Depression of the 1930s, philanthropic groups and municipal agencies helped to develop garden programs to feed the hungry by utilizing donated land and volunteer labor. In 1934, with the establishment of the Washington Emergency Relief Administration's Garden and Food Preservation program, many Seattleites were provided with seeds, garden plots, canning equipment, and advice to encourage food production for household consumption in order to offset unemployment and poverty (Saxe 1936). Seattle also had two work-relief garden programs that provided employment, including the Airport Farm, a fifty-five-acre site that employed fifty men and grew food that was distributed to charitable agencies (Leonard 1934).

3.5
Ballard High School victory garden, Seattle, 1943. Seattle Post-Intelligencer Collection, Museum of History and Industry, Seattle. All rights reserved.

3.6
An image of Picardo Farm.
Courtesy of City of Seattle,
P-Patch Program, n.d.

During World War II, Seattle joined the national effort to increase domestic food production through many victory gardens that were located in backyards, community gardens, parks, institutional grounds, college campuses, and elsewhere. There was a brief lull in community gardening during the 1950s and early 1960s, but interest soon resurfaced due to changing values related to the environment and community as well as the economic recession and rising oil prices.

The current community gardening movement in Seattle can be traced back to the early 1970s, when a group of students and families began a small community garden on the former three-acre Picardo Farm, which had been in production since the 1920s. In its first summer, 1971, the garden was cultivated by grade-school children to grow food for the Neighbors in Need program (Jensen 1988). The following year, with support from the Puget Consumer Cooperative (PCC), a community garden was established, with gardeners paying ten dollars for their plots and bringing their own water to the site. The owner, Rainie Picardo, let the group use the land free of charge, but given annual property taxes, he prepared to sell it in 1973. Public support ultimately resulted in the city council approving a lease of the land as an "experiment" in community gardening. Managed by PCC under the supervision of the Seattle Department of Parks and Recreation and the City Youth Department, the site was divided into 195 400-square-foot plots and 14 youth-service plots. The first year's harvest was celebrated with a vegetarian luncheon enjoyed by the mayor, the city council, and over sixty community gardeners and onlookers (Rea 1973).

The success of this effort was highlighted in newspaper articles and local newscasts. Almost immediately, city council members advocated for the "experiment"

3.7
Picardo P-Patch in 2007.
Photograph by Leslie Gia
Clark, 2007.

3.8
A P-Patch garden being
laid out. Courtesy of
City of Seattle, P-Patch
Program, n.d.

to expand to other sites and communities. A city council–appointed task force of citizens and city agency representatives was established to develop the P-Patch Program, a publicly administered organic community gardening program named after Picardo and undertaken by the Department of Human Resources. The program quickly expanded, with ten additional sites by 1974, of which eight were on city-owned property, one owned by the U.S. Postal Service, and one on land owned by a grocery store chain (*Seattle Times* 1974). In 1975, the city purchased the original P-Patch. That year, thirteen garden sites provided space for approximately 3,000 gardeners, who paid $7.50 for a ten-by-twenty-foot plot, with the city providing initial cultivation and furnishing fertilizer and water (Ammons 1975). Since then the P-Patch Program has continued to grow and evolve, with periods of struggle and growth. For instance, severe budget cuts in the early 1980s led to a reduction in services such as annual tilling and free fertilizer, and fees were raised, resulting in a temporary lull in participation and underutilized garden plots (Thorne 1983). Yet by 1992—twenty years after the P-Patch Program began—there were twenty-seven gardens totaling fourteen acres, and a waiting list of over 600 seeking plots (Ingle 1992). With a staff of two and many volunteers, the P-Patch Program not only maintained existing gardens and developed new gardens on a range of neighborhood sites but also established programs to donate food to foodbanks, provide education and job training to youth and the homeless, and extend services to the elderly and to new immigrants. The P-Patch Program was transferred to the Department of Neighborhoods in 1997, where it continues to operate today.

A WEB OF SUPPORT FOR COMMUNITY GARDENS

While each community garden relies on its immediate participants to undertake the planning and management of day-to-day and season-to-season needs, gardens also benefit from an expansive web of support that includes nonprofit organizations, governmental agencies, universities, schools, and local businesses. Support from nonprofit organizations ranges from specific technical advice given to an individual P-Patch to the facilitation of broader missions relating to urban agriculture, education, and assistance to low-income households. In some cases, gardening groups have formed themselves into nonprofit organizations in order to seek and manage funds, while others do not have this official status and instead work under the financial umbrella of other community nonprofit organizations. Additionally, the Washington State University (WSU) King County Extension program provides educational outreach, and students and faculty from local schools and universities have participated in the development and sustenance of Seattle's community gardens. The design-build studios at the University of Washington as well as several architecture and landscape architecture firms have also assisted in the design and development of a number of community gardens in the city. While some organizations provide general support available to all community garden groups, others specifically focus their resources on one site or constituency. This network of resources adds resiliency to community gardening groups through information and resources. The following provides brief descriptions of the key organizations.

P-Patch Program

The P-Patch Program is a staffed city program under the Seattle Department of Neighborhoods that facilitates the creation and maintenance of community, youth, and market gardens, with a fourth focus in food policy. Its citywide efforts include particular support for disadvantaged gardeners (Seattle Department of Neighborhoods 2007).

Through its Web site, staff presentations, and other means, the P-Patch Program provides general public information about how to start a community garden. Staff members help interested groups evaluate possible garden sites and assist in acquisition, working with both public and private landholders. As necessary, they help groups seeking funds to run special programs or help those who desire to purchase their garden sites to do so. The staff members also assist with soil testing, advising, and design process as appropriate. The P-Patch staff is responsible for the network of P-Patch gardens, providing assistance for managing the gardens and helping coordinate assistance from other agencies and organizations. The P-Patch staff manages applications of prospective gardeners and waiting lists, assigns plots, and resolves disputes. Staff members check each garden every month and assist garden coordinators as needed (Seattle Department of Neighborhoods 2006a).

As of 2006, the P-Patch Program oversees sixty-seven P-Patch community gardens located throughout the city. While the P-Patch Program assists all of these gardens, the actual gardens themselves and the programs they offer vary widely. Fifty of the P-Patch gardens are the more traditional allotment gardens in which gardeners have plots that they maintain individually, although many of these gardens have common areas and shared plots as well. Two gardens are communal gardens in which participants help maintain the entire site without individual plots. Thirteen of the P-Patch gardens are part of the Cultivating Communities program, and two are Cultivating Youth program gardens. As of 2007, P-Patch's "community gardens offer 2,500 plots [that] serve more than 6,000 urban gardeners on 23 acres of land" (Seattle Department of Neighborhoods 2007).

Any resident of Seattle may participate in a P-Patch community garden, although waiting lists for gardens in more densely populated areas may be discouraging, with waits of one and a half to three years. A gardener can apply for more than one preferred garden, and current participants have priority to renew and keep their own plots. Plots are leased on an annual basis and thus must be maintained for the full year. In 2007, annual fees ranged from thirty-four dollars per year for a ten-by-ten-foot plot to sixty-seven dollars per year for a ten-by-forty-foot plot, with support for those who qualify. These fees include the costs of water and organic fertilizers. Most gardens have some tools available for gardeners to use (Seattle Department of Neighborhoods 2007).

The P-Patch Program began with policies to promote organic gardening practices and has continued to require this. Gardeners cannot sell, but may donate their produce, and most P-Patches have special plots designated to grow produce for area food banks. These plots are planted and maintained collectively by garden volunteers, as are communal flower and herb beds that many P-Patch gardens contain. In addition to maintaining one's own plot and paths, each gardener must volunteer at least eight hours each year, for comunal parts of the P-Patch (Seattle Department of Neighborhoods 2007).

The essence of community gardening lies in the building of community along with the garden, and social events and communication support this. Each P-Patch holds a spring meeting, and gardeners assume responsibilities. A garden coordinator, or team of people, provide leadership and serve as a liaison to the P-Patch Program. An autumn harvest banquet brings together gardeners from across the city to share in a communal celebration.

P-Patch Trust (Formerly Friends of P-Patch)

In 1979, garden activists formed a nonprofit "P-Patch Advisory Council," which was restructured as a membership-based "Friends of P-Patch" in the 1990s. As a partner to the city-run P-Patch Program, the organization provides myriad support, including advocating for gardens, fundraising, supporting programs, and owning property. In 1987, the group was deeded its first permanent community garden, and it started a land acquisition fund in 1992. In 2003, the board of directors changed its articles of incorporation in order to become a community gardening land trust and changed its name to the P-Patch Trust (P-Patch Trust 2006). As of 2004, the Trust owned three P-Patches, portions of two P-Patches, and had acquired land for a future P-Patch. The P-Patch Trust serves as a fiscal agent for gardens, accounting for the expenditures of funds raised, and also provides insurance for P-Patch gardens. In addition to preserving gardens as permanent sites, the Trust advances community food security through support to the Cultivating Communities garden program at low-income housing, the Lettuce Link program that assists community gardens with donations to food banks, and a Gardenship fund for low-income gardeners' plot fees. The Trust also aids in communication by publishing the quarterly newsletter, the *P-Patch Post* (P-Patch Trust 2004).

Washington State University (WSU) King County Extension

Seattle was one of twenty-three cities to benefit from the Federal Urban Garden Program, run by the Department of Agriculture's cooperative extension service, which ran from 1976 to 1993 and added Seattle in 1985 (Lawson 2005). Its purpose was to promote urban gardening by establishing urban offices to provide educational opportunities and demonstration gardens. Although this program officially lost its funding in 1993, education and outreach efforts continue through WSU King County Extension. The WSU Extension started a Master Gardener program in King County in 1972 (WSU King County Extension 2007a). This program continues, as volunteers receive training and provide education and outreach addressing "environmentally safe gardening practices" (WSU King County Extension 2006).

The Master Gardener program has seven demonstration gardens in King County. WSU King County Extension also supports garden and food education through a program called Food Sense CHANGE (Cultivating Health and Nutrition through Garden Education), which serves low-income people through schools. This includes curriculum and experiential learning that occur through gardening (WSU King County Extension 2007b).

Seattle Tilth Association

Another local support is the nonprofit Seattle Tilth Association, formed in 1978 through efforts to secure the historic Home of the Good Shepherd site as a community center. Portions of the facility became Seattle Tilth's home, where programs, special events, a demonstration garden, and a children's garden are used for education and outreach. Seattle Tilth's activities include an annual plant sale and a harvest fair (Elliot and Peterson 2000). Besides the facility at the Home of the Good Shepherd, Seattle Tilth also operates a demonstration garden and offers workshops at Bradner Gardens Park, one of the case-study gardens included in this book (Seattle Tilth 2007).

Lettuce Link

The Lettuce Link program provides gardening information, seeds, and produce to Seattle's low-income families, as well as education on nutrition and growing food sustainably to children (Solid Ground 2007). Established in 1988 through a collaboration of the nonprofit Fremont Public Association, P-Patch Program, and WSU's

3.9
The food bank garden at Interbay P-Patch; community gardens are important contributors to local food banks through the Lettuce Link program. Photography by Leslie Gia Clark, 2007.

Extension food garden project, it is currently administered through the nonprofit Solid Ground, formerly the Fremont Public Association (Borba 1994). Lettuce Link works with P-Patch gardens to collect extra produce from individual gardeners and produce grown in "giving garden" plots and deliver it to local food banks. Additionally, Lettuce Link manages a three-quarter-acre garden and teaches children at Marra Farm, one of the case-study gardens described in this book. More than 41,000 pounds of organic produce was donated to the Lettuce Link program in 2006 (Lettuce Link 2006/2007).

Cultivating Communities / Seattle Housing Authority

In 1995, community gardens were established at Seattle Housing Authority (SHA) residential sites to enable healthy gardens for residents and to help build community. This program became known as the Cultivating Communities program, as a collaboration of the P-Patch Trust, P-Patch Program, and Seattle Housing Authority. Following the development of seven gardens that first year, more community

3.10
The Cultivating Communities garden with newly installed bed frames in High Point, Seattle, was developed as part of the HOPE VI housing redevelopment project by the Seattle Housing Authority. Photograph by Vanessa Lee, 2007.

gardens and two income-generating gardens were established over the next two years (Seattle Department of Neighborhoods 2006b). In 2006, there were thirteen Cultivating Communities gardens serving 163 plot holders (Macdonald 2006). The program supports various types of gardens that respond to respective community interests, including community gardens, senior gardens, and Community Supported Agriculture (CSA) gardens, with most gardeners having emigrated from Southeast Asia or East Africa (Cultivating Communities n.d.). CSA gardens connect gardeners with a group of consumers, who pay for a share of the harvest.

The Cultivating Youth project is a youth gardening and nutrition education program located on two garden sites. In 2006, there were 205 youth engaged in this project (Macdonald 2006). These gardening experiences provide youth with lessons on nutrition, fresh fruits and vegetables, and connection with their family cultures (Cultivating Communities n.d.).

Cultivating Communities has undertaken another initiative, the Neighborhood Food Access Project, to provide gardening outreach in low-income neighborhoods. This project has engaged Latino, African American, and East African residents in central and south Seattle, using interpreters and multilingual materials to involve non-English speakers. The project involves AmeriCorps VISTA (Volunteers in Service to America) members, who help to connect people with existing gardens, support building gardens, and foster leadership. VISTA members also work with Seattle Tilth Association and Seattle Public Utilities to create appropriate gardening classes for participants (Cultivating Communities n.d.).

SUPPORTIVE CITY AND NEIGHBORHOOD PLANNING

While many factors—climate, civic activism, engaged organizations, and others—have assured a community garden presence in Seattle, the inclusion of community gardening in planning efforts best expresses the commitment to support existing and future community gardens. In 1992, for instance, the city council passed Resolution 28610, which called for maintaining and expanding the P-Patch Program. This resolution recommended that P-Patches be part of the city's Comprehensive Plan and declared general support for community gardening and specific support for making surplus land available to gardening (Librizzi 1999). The 1994 comprehensive plan, entitled "Toward a Sustainable Seattle," located anticipated growth around existing neighborhood centers and provided amenities and services to support increased density. Among these, the plan established a target goal of one P-Patch per 2,500 households in these areas (Diers 2004). However, despite the many positive aspects of this plan, some community activists protested the lack of neighborhood self-determination in the planning process, ultimately leading the city to enable and fund a neighborhood-based participatory planning process for thirty-seven neighborhoods, including thirty-four "urban centers" or "urban villages" (Diers 2004). Although the process was time-consuming, by 1999 all the neighborhood-initiated plans had been approved and adopted by the city council. Interest and support for community gardening as a neighborhood activity was made evident by proposals for new community gardens in twenty of the neighborhood plans (Diers 2004). And as of 2006, the P-Patch Program has been involved in all but two of these twenty neighborhoods (Macdonald 2006).

An even clearer picture of citywide support for community garden expansion was developed through a five-year strategic plan, adopted by the city council in 2000. Noting that the annual waiting list for a plot included 600 to 800 people, this plan, proposed by the Friends of P-Patch and P-Patch Program, addressed the existing demand for more community gardens as well as the potential for future

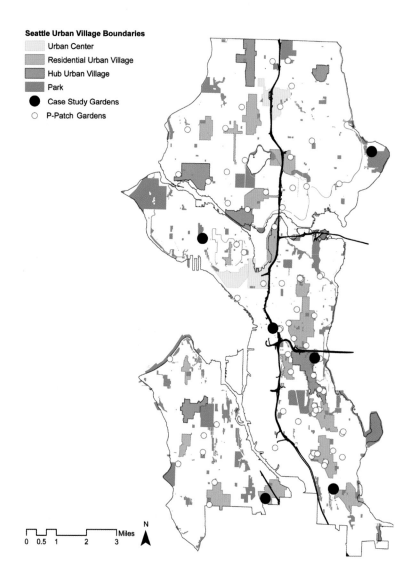

Seattle Urban Village Boundaries

- Urban Center
- Residential Urban Village
- Hub Urban Village
- Park
- ● Case Study Gardens
- ○ P-Patch Gardens

0 0.5 1   2   3   Miles

N

3.11
Map of locations of P-Patch gardens and Urban Village boundaries in Seattle. Map by Danielle Pierce, with data from City of Seattle.

projects as neighborhoods become denser as a result of planning and development efforts. Linking the benefits of community gardens with the values articulated in the Comprehensive Plan, the strategic plan called for fifteen to twenty new community gardens over a five-year period (with gardens to be located on city-owned land) and additional P-Patch staff to support this expansion. Three policy issues were identified: "(1) protection of current community gardens, (2) establishment of new community gardens, and (3) social equity and food security" (Seattle Legislative Information Service 2008). The city council supported the plan and made recommendations for its implementation.

COMMUNITY GARDEN DEVELOPMENT AND LAND TENURE

Guided by public interest, activism, and policies, efforts are underway to sustain existing community gardens and develop new gardens where they are needed. When the strategic plan was developed in 2000, twelve and a half of the thirty-nine P-Patches (not including the Cultivating Communities gardens) were owned by private individuals or organizations and thus were not secure (Seattle Legislative Information Service 2008). Efforts to protect garden sites have involved assigning permanent sites on public land and holding other properties through the P-Patch Trust. As of 2006, fifty-five of the sixty-seven P-Patch gardens are on land owned by city or county agencies or by the Seattle Housing Authority. The P-Patch Trust owns the land of three gardens entirely, parts of two gardens, and another parcel that is being developed as a P-Patch. Three gardens are on land owned by churches, two are owned by private low-income housing groups, and three occupy privately owned land. Efforts to create new gardens have surpassed the strategic plan's proposal (Macdonald 2006).

In addition to the P-Patch community gardens, gardens have also been established through community-based organizations, including the Danny Woo International District Community Garden, which is managed by the Inter*Im Community Development Association. Another example is El Centro de la Raza's Cesar Chavez Demonstration Garden, managed by the Master Gardener program. This garden serves as an educational and food resource, with produce used at El Centro (WSU King County Extension 2006).

While fewer of Seattle's P-Patch gardens are on leased private land, issues of stability and garden development remain in question for many gardens. P-Patch gardens do not have a designation in the city's land-use plan or zoning code, although this hasn't prevented locating gardens on sites where open space or parks are allowed. Seattle's Department of Parks and Recreation formally adopted a policy allowing P-Patch gardens in city parks in 2000 (Macdonald 2006). Whether on public or private land, the kind of land agreement impacts what services and resources the garden can provide. For instance, there are some agreements that may stipulate that no permanent structures can be built in the garden. Some agreements may not address the value of the soil condition, dismissing the sweat-equity aspect of improving the soil through composting and other amendments.

FUNDING PROGRAMS

As in other cities, Seattle's community gardens have been built and improved through the efforts of committed gardeners. Gardening groups often make the most of volunteer labor, in-kind contributions, and creative reuse of materials to develop their sites, but money is frequently needed as well. Fortunately, to realize their goals, Seattle's community gardeners may solicit support from various city funding programs and other grants. Several P-Patch gardens have received funds from the city's Neighborhood Matching Fund, which was initiated in 1989 to provide funding for diverse neighborhood projects. The funding requires a match from the community that can include community contribution of professional services, materials, volunteer labor, or cash. This program's budget grew from an initial $150,000 to $4.5 million in 2001, and was $3.2 million in 2006 (Diers 2004; Seattle Department of Neighborhoods 2006c).

Two of the Neighborhood Matching Fund types have been especially relevant to garden initiatives: the Small and Simple Projects Fund for projects taking six months or less, and the Large Projects Fund for projects taking up to one year. In 2006, the Small and Simple Projects Fund provided support for projects requesting up to $15,000, and that included planning and construction, and the Large Projects Fund provided up to $100,000. Applications to both funds are evaluated by the same weighted criteria: community benefit, participation, project feasibility, and match. The review process differs, as staff review and recommend Small and Simple Projects Fund applications with the approval of the director of the Department of Neighborhoods, and Large Projects Fund applications are reviewed by two citizen groups and require approval from the mayor and city council (Seattle Department of Neighborhoods 2006d, 2006e).

Another funding resource for community gardens has been the city's Pro Parks Levy. This fund was established in 2000 to help implement park and open-space plans developed in the neighborhood planning process. It also includes an Opportunity Fund to support unanticipated projects. Priority for the funds was given to underserved areas and areas receiving increased population. An application process and criteria for such projects were developed by the Pro Parks Levy Citizens Oversight Committee, which evaluates and recommends projects to the superintendent of Parks and Recreation. The superintendent forwards recommendations to the mayor and city council (Seattle Department of Parks and Recreation 2005). Since 2000, the Pro Parks Levy and its Opportunity Fund have supported the acquisition and/or development of several community gardens (Seattle Department of Parks and Recreation 2007b).

A CITY RIPE FOR COMMUNITY GARDENING

From its climate to its politics, Seattle stands out as an urban-garden-friendly community. Few other cities in the United States have the same degree of public support in place—dedicated public departments, nonprofit organizations, and public funding sources—to enable urban gardening to shift from being viewed as an interim or temporary use of vacant land to becoming a permanent public resource and amenity. As a result, the urban community gardens in Seattle provide important lessons in programming and site design to encourage long-term use and public participation. While the gardens are as individualized and expressive as their neighborhoods and the people who participate in them, together they convey a green network and green way of thinking that is as much shaped by local conditions as it is shaping Seattle itself.

SEATTLE CASE STUDIES

Every community garden is distinctive due to context, participation, and programming. As such, it is difficult to provide case studies that represent community gardens in all situations. In many ways, Seattle's community gardens are unique, and conclusions drawn from examples here may or may not apply to other cities and regions. However, the variety of Seattle's community gardens provides some important themes, lessons, and suggestions that can be adapted to local conditions. To illustrate the range of contexts, issues, and approaches of community gardens in Seattle, we selected six gardens to develop the case studies. The age, location, participants, and programs detailed in the case studies provide insights into the many roles that community gardens play, as well as their versatility in meeting the changing needs of the communities they serve.

The case studies are arranged chronologically, from the oldest to the most recently built gardens. This structure reveals not only how much change can occur within a garden over time but also shifting ideas about the public nature and programmatic opportunities in newer community gardens. Each case study reflects the varying socioeconomic and land-use contexts within the city, the demographics of participants, the appearance of the gardens, and the functions they serve. Each case was chosen for a particular theme:

- Interbay P-Patch: Originally established in 1974, this community garden is known for its participant activism in light of its three locations on a capped landfill and necessary soil-building efforts.
- Thistle P-Patch: Started in 1974, this garden has evolved with the chang-

ing demographics of South Seattle and now serves as an economic resource for immigrants and refugees.

- Danny Woo International District Community Garden: Established in 1976, this garden (not run through the P-Patch program) serves an immigrant community and primarily elderly populations.

- Bradner Gardens Park: Established in 1995, this garden is an artful hybrid space that includes both P-Patch and park features and is facing gentrification concerns.

- Marra Farm: Established in 1997, this urban farm provides food, educational, and income-generating garden programs involving a coalition of public and nonprofit agencies.

- Magnuson Community Garden: Established in 2001 within a large metropolitan park, this garden provides a wide range of spaces and programs to encourage public use and participation.

While the gardens are distinct, a common framework is used to examine the cases in order to afford comparisons and a broader perspective on community gardens. Each case study is organized as a chapter with the following headings:

Tour of the Garden

Background and History

Design Process and Implementation

Funding and Support

Organization and Participation

Programs and Functions

Contextual Factors and Challenges

In addition, unique features that may not be present in other gardens are described in a "Special Lesson" section at the end of each chapter.

Information was collected from a wide range of sources, including writ-

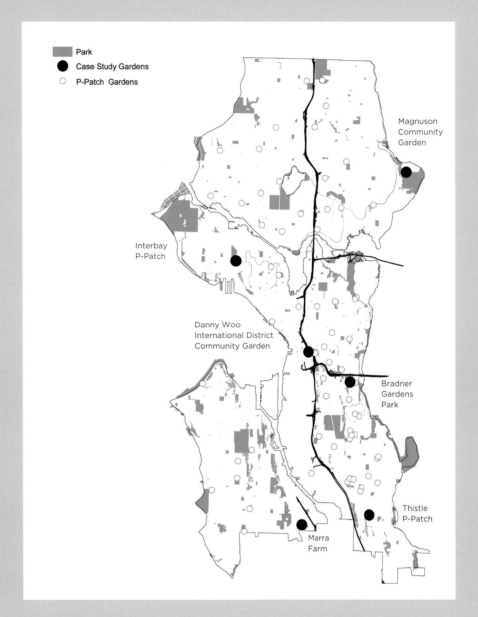

Park

Case Study Gardens

P-Patch Gardens

Magnuson
Community
Garden

Interbay
P-Patch

Danny Woo
International District
Community Garden

Bradner
Gardens
Park

Thistle
P-Patch

Marra
Farm

II.1
Locations of case-study
gardens in Seattle. Map
by Nathan Brightbill and
Leslie Gia Clark, with data
from City of Seattle.

ten materials, site visits, and interviews with organizers and gardeners. In
addition to published materials, public documents, and local newspaper
articles, information was collected from more ephemeral sources, such as
the *P-Patch Post* and newsletters and information sheets from the individual gardens. Expert interviews included past and present staff of P-Patch,
P-Patch Trust, and other organizations, as well as garden coordinators,

volunteers, longtime participants, and designers involved in these gardens. Through multiple site visits, the individual gardens were mapped and analyzed. The resulting case studies outline the development and evolution of the gardens. They also provide a snapshot of garden design, programming, and participation as it existed in 2006, with full acknowledgement that the gardens will continue to evolve.

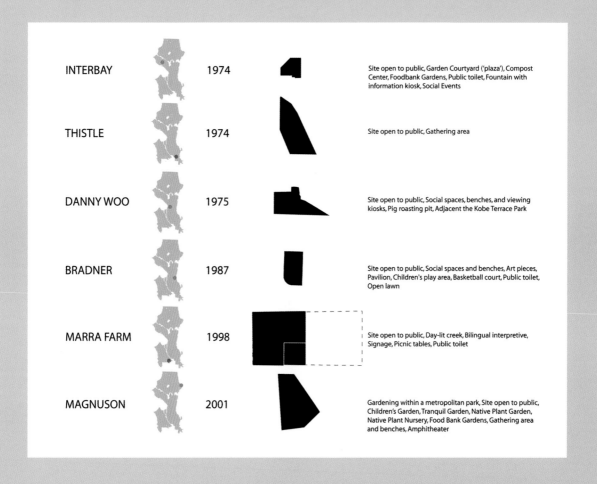

INTERBAY 1974 — Site open to public, Garden Courtyard ('plaza'), Compost Center, Foodbank Gardens, Public toilet, Fountain with information kiosk, Social Events

THISTLE 1974 — Site open to public, Gathering area

DANNY WOO 1975 — Site open to public, Social spaces, benches, and viewing kiosks, Pig roasting pit, Adjacent the Kobe Terrace Park

BRADNER 1987 — Site open to public, Social spaces and benches, Art pieces, Pavilion, Children's play area, Basketball court, Public toilet, Open lawn

MARRA FARM 1998 — Site open to public, Day-lit creek, Bilingual interpretive, Signage, Picnic tables, Public toilet

MAGNUSON 2001 — Gardening within a metropolitan park, Site open to public, Children's Garden, Tranquil Garden, Native Plant Garden, Native Plant Nursery, Food Bank Gardens, Gathering area and benches, Amphitheater

4

Interbay P-Patch

LOCATION: 15th Avenue West and West Armour Street, Seattle

ESTABLISHED: 1974

CONSTRUCTED/REBUILT: 1974, 1992, 1997 (three site locations)

DESIGNER(S): P-Patch and gardeners (Interbay 1 and 2 design); gardeners working with city senior landscape architect Joe Neiford (Interbay 3 design); CAST Architecture with gardeners (community shed and kiosk design and build)

MANAGED BY: Seattle Department of Neighborhoods' P-Patch Program and Interbay P-Patch leadership team

SITE OWNERSHIP(S): Seattle Department of Parks and Recreation

LEASE/OWNERSHIP TERMS: agreement with Seattle Department of Parks and Recreation

SIZE: 1 acre

NUMBER OF PLOTS: 132 (Seattle Department of Neighborhoods 2005)

NEIGHBORHOOD STATISTICS: Interbay neighborhood. Located between two neighborhoods:

QUEEN ANNE: Population 26, 595, with median household income of $50,047. Ethnic/racial composition: 85% white; 5% Asian; 3% Latino/Hispanic; 2% Black; 2% multiracial; 1% other (*Seattle Post-Intelligencer* 2006a)

MAGNOLIA: Population 21,579, with median household income of $58,288. Ethnic/racial composition: 85% white; 6% Native Hawaiian/Pacific Islander; 4% Hispanic/Latino; 1% black; 1% American Indian/Alaska Native; 3% other (*Seattle-Post Intelligencer* 2006b)

TOUR OF INTERBAY P-PATCH

With a landscaped berm and an orchard separating the Interbay P-Patch from its adjacent busy commercial street, a visitor may not be prepared for the abundant vitality of the garden hidden within. The garden fronts 15th Avenue West, an arterial that links downtown Seattle to neighborhoods to the north. The towering fence of an adjacent golf course frames the garden's edges to the west and north, and the southern side meets a steep slope of blackberries and a dead-end street. Thus, access is only available at two areas: an ornamental gate at the southeast corner, and the parking area along the northeastern boundary, where a trellis entry and a gate invite one out of the car and onto garden paths. Looking back across the parking area towards the street, one sees a bunker area for large deliveries of organic debris and the shed for food bank donations.

When entering from the southeast corner, one navigates by way of an orthogonal layout of paths with garden-inspired names, such as Dahlia Way or Huckleberry Lane. Plots to either side reveal a range of plants and aesthetics, from the highly productive food bank plots, which are planted to maximize harvest and volunteer ease, to individual's plots, which may have fanciful edging, pavers, and statuary.

4.1
With a golf course flanking it, the Interbay P-Patch faces a major commercial street and the Queen Anne neighborhood. Map by Nathan Brightbill, with data from City of Seattle.

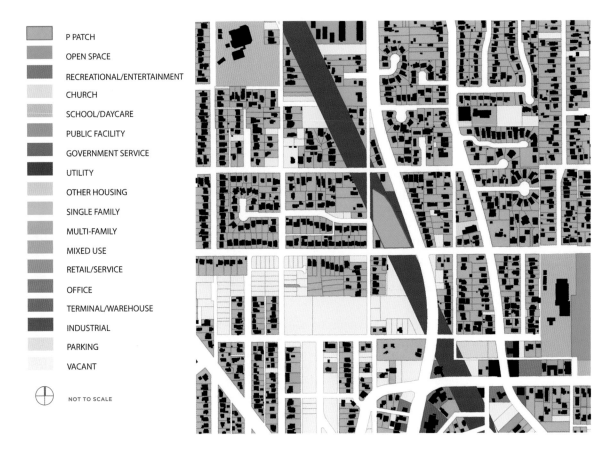

P PATCH

OPEN SPACE

RECREATIONAL/ENTERTAINMENT

CHURCH

SCHOOL/DAYCARE

PUBLIC FACILITY

GOVERNMENT SERVICE

UTILITY

OTHER HOUSING

SINGLE FAMILY

MULTI-FAMILY

MIXED USE

RETAIL/SERVICE

OFFICE

TERMINAL/WAREHOUSE

INDUSTRIAL

PARKING

VACANT

NOT TO SCALE

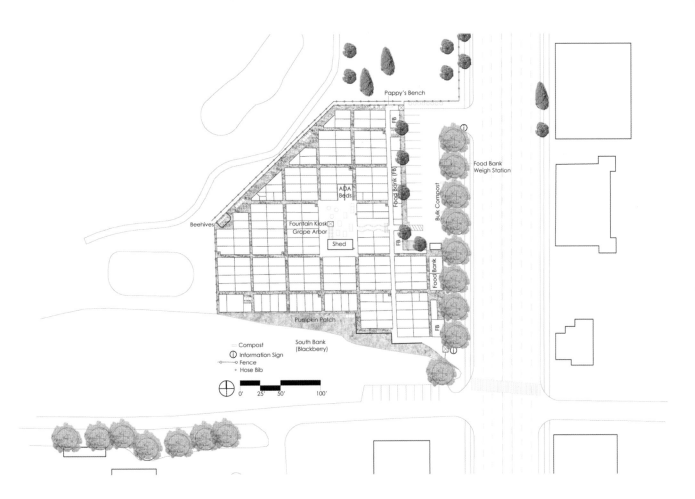

Pappy's Bench

FB

Food Bank (FB)

ADA Beds

Bulk Compost

Food Bank Weigh Station

FB

Fountain Kiosk
Grape Arbor
Shed

Beehives

Food Bank

FB

Pumpkin Patch

South Bank
(Blackberry)

☐ Compost
① Information Sign
○—○ Fence
+ Hose Bib

0'   25'   50'   100'

4.2
Existing site plan of the
Interbay P-Patch. Drawing
by Nathan Brightbill.

4.3
The Interbay P-Patch is
an oasis along a predomi-
nantly industrial corridor,
with the Queen Anne
neighborhood looking
over it. Photograph by
Leslie Gia Clark, 2007.

4.4
A marker indicates the
path names. Photograph
by Leslie Gia Clark, 2007

Visible throughout the relatively flat garden is the central plaza area, marked by a
shed with a dramatic swooped roofline. This area draws the visitor into the heart
of the garden, where one is sure to find other people. A lucky visitor will stop by
during one of the garden's famous social events and have a chance to partake in the
garden harvest. At other times, the central plaza is the site for meetings to discuss
garden upkeep.

BACKGROUND AND HISTORY: BUILDING COMMUNITY THROUGH ADVERSITY

The current appearance of this verdant oasis belies the dislocations that the gardeners have experienced. The original Interbay P-Patch was established in 1974
atop part of a clay-capped landfill (Seattle Department of Neighborhoods 2005).
Given this context, the first task was to create rich soil. While gardeners worked
the garden, the city made plans to use the landfill for a golf course. In 1981, gardeners petitioned the city council for one acre of the site to remain a community
P-Patch, and a resolution was passed (B. Swee 2005). This resolution, however, did
not protect the location of the P-Patch. In 1992, the gardeners set about establishing "Interbay 2" by relocating their soil, establishing paths, and replanting with
raised beds. Compost bins and a toolshed were built, and a food bank area was
created. When told in 1997 that the P-Patch had to move again, given new plans
for the golf course, the gardeners had developed political savvy. The resulting city
council resolution stated that the new location would be about the same size, that
"the reconfigured garden [be] equal to or better than the existing garden in terms
of improved irrigation and drainage systems, uniform 18" depth of quality topsoil

4.5
Located next to a municipal golf course, Interbay P-Patch was moved twice before settling in its current location. Photograph by Vanessa Lee, 2005.

and 3 foot wide paths," and that assistance in the relocation and lumber to create beds would be provided (B. Swee 2005; City of Seattle Legislative Information Service 2008). "Interbay 3" was developed with assistance from the Parks Department horticulture staff and was officially dedicated in August 1997 (Schutte 1997a, 1997b). It has continued to evolve through the efforts of the gardeners and through the support of the Neighborhood Matching Fund, which has allowed the development of features such as the garden's bamboo trellis, berm edge, and shed (B. Swee 2005).

Rather than diminishing the garden's viability, the struggle to sustain the garden through two relocations has built a stronger community (Deneen 2000). Indeed, this P-Patch is renowned as a sociable and welcoming community of gardeners. Regular events bring gardeners and others together for gardening, food, and conversation. The gardeners welcome visitors from schools, from the local area, and from around the world.

DESIGN PROCESS AND IMPLEMENTATION: DESIGN FOR EFFICIENCY AND SOCIAL ACTIVITY

Having already developed two garden sites, the Interbay gardeners were veterans in consideration of site and gardener needs when they began working on a new design for Interbay 3. A gardener recalled how the initial site plan was developed through design meetings, with construction drawings developed by city senior landscape architect Joe Neiford. The result reflects shared utilitarian needs, efficient circulation and plot allocation, and a desire for a social core. At the edges of the site are

4.6
The kitchen/tool shed designed by CAST Architecture, along with the plaza area, serves as the focal point and gathering space in the garden. Photograph by Vanessa Lee, 2005.

4.7
The information kiosk in the garden courtyard is also an ecorevelatory design for capturing rainwater. Photograph by Vanessa Lee, 2005.

located the utilitarian functions that require street access, such as a limited parking area, compost and mulch storage, and commonly maintained food bank garden plots. The noise and chaos from the adjacent arterial road are buffered by a berm that is planted with fruit trees. The garden is accessed by entrance gateways with plantings. Given the large, flat site, the orthogonal layout of paths and plots maximizes gardening space and access. Orientation is facilitated through a path-naming system, with east-west paths called ways, with floral designations such as "Dahlia Way" and "Tulip Way," while north-south paths are berry lanes, such as "Huckleberry Lane" and "Raspberry Lane" (B. Swee 2005). The garden plots are divided into four geographic blocks, each black with its own name. Compost bins and irrigation connections are distributed across the site. The P-Patch includes garden beds designed for handicapped accessibility (Seattle Department of Neighborhoods 2005).

The physical and social center of the garden is the "garden courtyard," which includes a shed, courtyard, and grape arbor. As described by one of the people involved in its design, it is "almost like a traditional urban plaza with the backdrop being the community garden." The shed, with its high-profile, overhanging roof, serves as both a landmark that is visible throughout the garden and a place for storing common equipment and preparing meals. In the plaza framed by the shed and arbor, many social events are held. Solar-powered lighting allows for these events to linger into the evening hours (Alexander 2004). The shed was a community-based planning and construction effort supported by the Small and Simple Projects Fund and CAST Architecture (C. Swee 2003).

To facilitate communication, the P-Patch recently created a new kiosk on the west side of the plaza. A committee was formed to work on the design with CAST Architecture, and the design was presented for a vote at a meeting of all the gardeners. The kiosk contains a history of the garden, a fountain with a solar battery and circulating pump, and a bulletin board.

Not to be taken for granted is the inclusion of toilet facilities within the garden. This is a particularly appropriate feature given the size of the garden and the fact that most of the gardeners do not live nearby. The group leases a port-a-potty, which is located next to a greenhouse by the garden's parking area.

FUNDING AND SUPPORT: CREATIVE REUSE

The Interbay gardeners have been successful at leveraging local funding with volunteer efforts and donations, as well as creatively using in-kind and recycled materials. The Interbay 2 garden included the construction of a toolshed and compost bins with support from the Neighborhood Matching Fund. Following the garden's 1997 relocation as Interbay 3, gardeners received Neighborhood Matching Fund support in 1998 to construct a bamboo entry arbor that was designed and built by a Cambodian temple artist. Another such award in 2000 provided funds to support construction of a rock wall for the berm and an irrigation system for the berm and food bank garden. And in 2002, this program supported the development of the multiuse shed that has become the hearth of this active garden(B. Swee 2005). More recently, a Starbucks Make Your Mark grant was secured for the kiosk (Macdonald 2004a).

The Interbay P-Patch epitomizes the community-building goals of the Neighborhood Matching Fund program through the garden's planning and design process and through the creative leveraging of funds with volunteerism and in-kind donations. This is well illustrated in the development of the shed. With limited funding from the Neighborhood Matching Fund, much of the shed's materials were donated or purchased at a discount. The design and construction process was led by a former gardener who was an architect with CAST Architecture. The firm donated its time, as did an engineering firm, to the design of a dramatic but uncomplicated structure that could be built with volunteers. Gardeners contributed design ideas, and when it came time to build, many participated with CAST members continuing to donate their time in what one of the people involved in the design called "a barn-raising-style work party." One gardener remarked, "Over 60 percent of the gardeners in this garden spent hours at a time in constructing this toolshed."

Some of the garden's features are a result of unique opportunities to reuse materials gathered from around the city. For instance, the garden entry trellises are made from the metal frames that used to ornament the city's port-a-potties in the downtown area. An opportunity to reuse a flagpole from the Seattle Center Flag Pavilion led to the development of a gardener-designed flag that marks the site. The garden's beehive structure is from a previous Interbay P-Patch shed. One gardener declared, "Almost everything is recycled. . . . It's part of the aesthetic of being organic; it's part of the aesthetic of being a community garden open space." The garden has also benefited from individual donations. The shed's solar panel and batteries were donated by a gardener (Alexander 2004). A nearby family donated a small greenhouse to the garden (B. Swee 2005).

Fundraising events such as the annual salmon barbeque are often opportunities to celebrate together. Other fundraising efforts have included a biennial dahlia sale and the sale of the honey produced by the garden's bees (C. Swee 2003).

4.8
This entry trellis once served as a frame for a downtown portable toilet. Photograph by Vanessa Lee, 2005.

ORGANIZATION AND PARTICIPATION: TEAM LEADERSHIP

While the Interbay P-Patch was initially organized along the lines of the city's other P-Patches, with a volunteer coordinator, Interbay's extensive programs and activities benefit from having a team of people. In 2002 the group increased their organizational capacity by creating a leadership team to coordinate the garden's facilities and activities. The team includes leaders from each of the four P-Patch garden blocks, beekeepers, and a treasurer, community liaison, and chipper/shredder coordinator, and leaders for facilities, communications, community gardens, good neighbors and hospitality, education, composting, and the food bank garden (which also has an assistant team leader). Two of these members also serve as cochairs for the leadership team. With the garden organized into four blocks, each block has leaders who oversee "good neighbor issues," such as helping when a gardener is sick or on vacation and resolving conflicts between neighboring gardening plots (B. Swee 2005). While Interbay has not been immune to conflict, the gardeners have managed to establish an approach that seems to work. As one gardener comments, "Every community has some conflict, and if you follow standard processes to resolve them, it works pretty well."

The city's P-Patch Program and nonprofit P-Patch Trust also play a role in supporting the garden. The P-Patch Program provides support for site management, including monitoring that plots are maintained. The Trust has advocated for the garden to the city council, provided tools through its tool fund, and operated as the fiscal agent for Department of Neighborhoods grant projects at Interbay (B. Swee 2005).

PROGRAMS AND FUNCTIONS: CELEBRATING GARDEN AND COMMUNITY

As a P-Patch, Interbay provides much more than gardening plots for individuals. It serves as a hub of community life for gardeners and visitors alike, offering traditions of work and fun, as well as education, service, and outreach.

P-Patch Garden

Well, our youngest gardener is about a year old, maybe a little older. And our oldest is ninety. And we have everything in between.
—A GARDENER

Since the garden is located in an industrial swath of land and is adjacent to two neighborhoods, it draws in many people who drive or bike to get to the garden. The garden serves a diverse community, with a range of economic and ethnic backgrounds, ages, and abilities. Some gardeners live in the adjacent neighborhoods, and others come from the farther reaches of Seattle.

This garden appeals to people for a variety of reasons. For some, it is the garden's size and features that draw them; for others, the social nature of the garden is welcomed. As one gardener described choosing the Interbay P-Patch, "It seemed to have a critical mass of people: with 130 or so gardeners, there is almost always someone else in the garden to chat with and compare notes." When asked about what is most enjoyable about Interbay, one gardener responded, "Gosh, do I have to choose one thing? . . . Everything about it is enjoyable and satisfying, but I think that the community at this garden is another really important part of the gardening experience. The fresh air. And it's peaceful. We have so many species of bees. We have butterflies, hummingbirds. We think there are goldfinches that are nesting here. . . . It's an oasis in the middle of the city."

Social and Learning Events

We go to work and meet people at our work, but the garden gives [us] another community to be involved in. . . . The community in the garden is just another outlet. A social place.
—A GARDENER

Interbay's reputation as a social garden draws from traditions in the garden that blend work, learning, and socializing. These traditions include events such as Friday night potlucks and "compost socials"—work parties on Saturday mornings, with soup served for lunch (Schutte 1999a). Training is provided for pruning orchard trees on the berm, and compost workshops are offered (B. Swee 2005). Preschool, high school, and garden groups visit the garden. Celebrations include an annual salmon barbeque, started in 1999, and seasonal gatherings such as a wreath-making party and New Year's dinner (Schutte 1999a; C. Swee 2003). A gardener described several events, such as a solstice party and Fourth of July party. In 2004, a "Jazz in the Garden" fundraising event and a "Big Fat Greek Picnic and Dance" were held (Macdonald 2004a, 2004b).

Garden Tourism

A unique community green space in the area, Interbay P-Patch seems to thrive as a magnet for gardeners and visitors alike. One gardener noted, "There are more non-gardeners involved in the food bank than there are gardeners. And there are some nongardener regulars at the Friday night potlucks. There are people who just enjoy being here."

Gardeners observe that Interbay has been a destination for photographers—including filming for a local television program and for a retail catalogue. In 1999, two gardeners held their wedding in the garden, with a compost class underway nearby (Deneen 2000). One year, the garden's guestbook had entries by 514 guests from around the state, the country, and the globe. One visitor wrote, "A Paradise close to Earth!" while another noted, "You are all saving the planet. Thank you for your inspiration." Neighbors "just jogging past" have discovered the garden as well and expressed appreciation (Sexton 2001).

Composting and Soil Programs

Given its initial poor soil conditions, the Interbay P-Patch became very active in and renowned for composting and soil development. The site supports the delivery of leaves from the city and grass clippings from organic landscape contractors to a large bunker area resulting in "tons of organic compost"

4.9
Celebrity Compost bins feature local and national figures, including former Seattle mayor Paul Schell. Photograph by Vanessa Lee, 2005.

(B. Swee 2005, 2). In addition, some thirty compost bins are located around the garden in which gardeners may leave their debris. Education on building healthy soil has been the focus of several activities, including a demonstration garden, workshops, an exchange with Southeast Asian P-Patch gardeners, and a "Celebrity Compost" program in which local and national figures turn compost bins that are then named for them (Schutte 1999b; B. Swee 2005; Schutte and Phelan 2000; Rowley 1998).

Food Bank Garden

Many P-Patches include areas for volunteers to grow food for local food banks, but Interbay is exceptional in this sense. A team leader and assistant team leader coordinate over 2,000 square feet of garden space, as well as compost and worm bins, that are devoted to food bank gardening (B. Swee 2005; Hucka 2002). The food bank garden and donations from P-Patch gardeners have supplied 4,000 to 5,000 pounds of organic produce annually to the local Lettuce Link program (Lovejoy 2004; Hucka 2002).

The food bank garden also provides a valuable source of outreach and education. Between April and October, weekly work parties are held to care for these gardens, and volunteers are welcome to help in this effort and to learn organic gardening (Hucka 2002). Plants are identified with labels and instructions, which provides informal learning opportunities. More formal learning opportunities are in place with a local high school and as a service-learning option for students in the Community Environment and Planning program at the University of Washington (B.

4.10
Food bank gardens include signs on plant needs. Photograph by Leslie Gia Clark, 2007.

Swee 2005). A horticulture teacher at Ballard High School connected the students' curriculum with the food bank garden; the class grows plant starts for the food bank garden and makes weekly trips to the garden to plant and observe the results (Cropp 2005).

Common Gardens

Common garden spaces, such as the berm, the orchard, the entry gardens, and the plantings along the parking lot, are maintained by a community garden team and leader. Training is provided for pruning orchard trees, and work parties are held twice a week (B. Swee 2005).

Beekeeping

Another essential activity at Interbay involves honeybees, with honey sold for fundraising. Three hives were cared for in 2003, with the beekeepers moving the bees to the mountains in the summer for fireweed (C. Swee 2003). In 2005, the leadership changed, with three keepers caring for two hives (B. Swee 2005).

CONTEXTUAL FACTORS AND CHALLENGES: PROBLEMS OF PILFERING

But...that's the reality. You're gonna have a certain amount of theft in the garden. . . . My only problem is when they [thieves] don't know how to harvest. So they ruin the plant, when there's something more that can be gotten from it.

—A GARDENER

The lack of active adjacent land uses makes the Interbay site vulnerable to the same misuse that plagues many urban open spaces, notably problems with illegal dumping and theft. A range of theft-deterring strategies have been undertaken. One gardener tries to obscure the more valued crops, such as tomatoes, at the center of their plots while distracting would-be thieves with less desirable plantings along the plot's periphery. Another gardener resorted to staking out the garden and was able to contact the police when he spotted a thief (B. Swee 2000). Some pilfering is attributed to a nearby camp of homeless people who visit the garden and use the toilet. Addressing the homeless occupation of the garden has been an ongoing concern. At one point, rather than discourage the homeless in the garden, the garden leaders attempted to encourage their active participation by providing one homeless man with a plot (Saul 2000). However, this approach requires familiarity and relationship building.

4.11
With its adjacent municipal golf course and bordering arterial street, Interbay P-Patch is isolated from neighborhood activities. Photograph by Leslie Gia Clark, 2007.

SPECIAL LESSON: EXPANDING BEYOND THE GARDEN TO HELP OTHERS

The community engagement at Interbay extends beyond the garden through its social, educational, and outreach activities. For example, Interbay's tradition of growing food for those in need remains a focus as the active food bank gardens and gardeners provide substantial donations (B. Swee 2005).

Interbay's engagement also extended beyond the local community in the wake of the September 11 terrorist attacks in New York City, when it used its composting facilities in a gesture of healing. After the tragic event, the Seattle Center's International Fountain became the civic focus for mourning as mounds of flowers and wishes were placed there. Later, the flowers were moved to Interbay, where hundreds of volunteers separated the flowers from the noncompostable materials. Eighty cubic yards of flowers were mixed with donated brown organic matter. One gardener suggested giving a portion of the compost to the community garden nearest the attack site, and this vision was realized a year later. "Million-flower compost" was delivered to the Liberty Community Garden in Manhattan, where representatives from the Interbay P-Patch and others took part in the rededication ceremony on September 28, 2002 (Thorness 2002; Rowley 2002).

As a community garden, Interbay demonstrates how the process of gardening becomes a medium for connecting people in myriad ways, resulting in abundant benefits.

5

Thistle P-Patch

LOCATION: Martin Luther King Jr. Way and Cloverdale Street, Seattle

ESTABLISHED: 1974

CONSTRUCTED/REBUILT: 2004 (most recently)

DESIGNER(S): Brook Sullivan (AmeriCorps volunteer) and Julie Bryant (P-Patch staff)

MANAGED BY: Seattle Department of Neighborhoods P-Patch Program

OTHER PARTNERS: WSU King County Extension

SITE OWNERSHIP(S): Seattle City Light

LEASE/OWNERSHIP TERMS: temporary-use permit

SIZE: 3.5 acres

NUMBER OF PLOTS: 160 (each 10 x 40 feet; Seattle Department of Neighborhoods 2008)

NEIGHBORHOOD STATISTICS: Rainier Valley neighborhood. Population 37,056, with median household income of $44,259. Ethnic/racial composition: 30% white; 29% black; 29% Asian; 6% Hispanic/Latino; 1% American Indian/Alaska Native; 1% Native Hawaiian/Pacific Islander; 4% other (*Seattle Post-Intelligencer* 2006)

TOUR OF THISTLE P-PATCH

Located in a utility easement under high-tension power lines, the Thistle P-Patch is an unexpected oasis amid heavy-traffic roadways and utility infrastructure. A resi-

▢	P PATCH
▢	OPEN SPACE
▢	RECREATIONAL/ENTERTAINMENT
▢	CHURCH
▢	SCHOOL/DAYCARE
▢	PUBLIC FACILITY
▢	GOVERNMENT SERVICE
▢	UTILITY
▢	OTHER HOUSING
▢	SINGLE FAMILY
▢	MULTI-FAMILY
▢	MIXED USE
▢	RETAIL/SERVICE
▢	OFFICE
▢	TERMINAL/WAREHOUSE
▢	INDUSTRIAL
▢	PARKING
▢	VACANT

⊕ NOT TO SCALE

5.1
The Thistle P-Patch
is located in a utility
easement in Rainier
Valley, southeast of
downtown Seattle. Map
by Nathan Brightbill,
with data from City of
Seattle.

dential neighborhood looks down over the garden from the hill above. Despite its developed urban setting, the lush garden is a reminder that this area of the Rainier Valley provides rich bottomland soil that serves as a good foundation for a garden. And that is critical to this P-Patch garden, where productivity is paramount. The main access off a side road is marked by a gate and a dirt parking area. A newly installed wooden fence surrounds the gardens. The garden's narrow paths are just wide enough for a wheelbarrow. On both sides of the paths, the grid of garden plots is revealed through gardener-made borders and disparate planting plans. It is readily apparent that the gardeners here are practicing gardening traditions that differ from the stereotypical vegetable garden plot. The predominantly Asian gardeners are revealing the farming and gardening traditions of Thailand, Cambodia, Laos, Korea, Vietnam, and elsewhere. Sticks, lumber, rebar, and other objects serve as apparatuses for climbing beans and other plants. The garden is a sea of lush plants and vegetables, including corn, peas, squash, cilantro, beans, onions, winter mustard, kale, broccoli, radishes, mint, chard, lettuce, chives, garlic, watercress, tomatoes, Korean celery, peppers, and medicinal plants (Macdonald 2004). Crops are often intermixed to take full advantage of growing seasons and to maximize the limited space of the plots.

Main
Entrance

Light Rail 2009

Chief Sealth Bike Trail

Powerline Easement

+ Hose Bib
ⓘ Information Sign

0'   25'   50'   100'

5.2
Site plan of Thistle
P-Patch. Drawing by
Nathan Brightbill

BACKGROUND AND HISTORY: FORGOTTEN
AND REDISCOVERED

Established in 1974 in the Rainier Valley in southeast Seattle, the Thistle P-Patch
garden is one of the oldest P-Patch gardens in the city today. As such, it has gone
through changes that largely reflect the larger community's demographic, eco-

5.3
With gardens under the power lines, the Thistle P-Patch transforms a utility corridor into productive land. Photograph by Leslie Gia Clark, 2007.

nomic, and transportation shifts. For instance, during the 1970s, as the community experienced economic decline and population loss, the garden was underutilized and somewhat stagnant. Through the 1980s and 1990s, an influx of immigrants and refugees began to bring changes and new vitality to this struggling area in South Seattle. Today, Rainier Valley is the most racially diverse neighborhood in Seattle, with African American and Asian residents making up 60 percent of the area's population. New Asian mini-malls have taken over vacant and struggling businesses to serve the valley's new Vietnamese, Cambodian, and Laotian residents. The P-Patch also went through a rebirth, as immigrant and refugee gardeners discovered the weedy, underutilized garden site and transformed it into a working and thriving urban community garden. With forty plots in the early 1980s, the garden grew steadily in the 1990s but was still not big enough to meet the demand. A redesign in 2004 reorganized the footpaths and equalized the plot sizes. Today, there are 160 plots serving primarily low-income immigrant and refugee families from East and Southeast Asia.

DESIGN PROCESS AND IMPLEMENTATION: MAXIMIZING GARDEN PRODUCTIVITY

I don't think it's brain science at a P-Patch, and I think it really needs to come out of the people.
—A FORMER GARDENER

During the first thirty years of the Thistle P-Patch garden's existence, the site was roughly platted into garden plots of varying sizes. As its use intensified, problems with poor drainage and differing plot sizes, and disputes over boundaries and edges emerged. As one gardener recalls, tensions grew to the extent that some gardeners "sabotaged each other's gardens, complaining back and forth." In 2004, the P-Patch Program initiated a redesign process. The design process revealed some distinct needs and challenges in the garden. During the course of three meetings, gardeners described their desires for better water access, a fence, wider paths, and parking (Macdonald 2002). In addition to serving the gardeners' interests, the design also had to address restrictions imposed by easements from power lines, a bike path, a city street, and gas pipelines. As one of the designers recalls, the gardeners were not generally interested in anything other than practical improvements: "It was kind of like, whatever you do is great. . . . To them, it was like, what do we need this for? We could just build this on our own. We just want to make new plots and get to gardening." The resulting design expanded the gardening area, equalized plot sizes, improved the water system, and delineated common paths.

Unlike many P-Patches, Thistle does not have common areas or social amenities. Because gardeners wanted to maximize gardening space and did not feel the need for a social center, the design does not include any gathering place. As one volunteer recalls, "At

5.4
Realignment of paths and plots provide access and equalize plot areas for the gardeners. Photograph by Arielle Farina Clark, 2005.

5.5
Intensity of uses and problems of theft and vandalism resulted in heavily guarded borders between plots. Photograph by Arielle Farina Clark, 2005.

first we were kind of going for a gathering formal entry kind of thing and that ended up totally getting squashed by the gardeners." Although P-Patch sets a standard of three-foot widths for paths in order to provide public access, the gardeners at Thistle wanted narrower paths in order to maximize gardening space.

Whereas the toolshed often serves as a de facto social space in other P-Patches, Thistle is distinct in not even having a common toolshed or space. This has partly to do with a stipulation from the site owner, Seattle City Light, which does not allow building in the utility corridor. But it also has to do with the security concerns of the gardeners, who do not trust the neighborhood. As a result, some of the gardeners have built low storage sheds, while others bring their tools to the site.

The different gardening practices of the gardeners also influenced the site plan. For example, there is no composting area because it is not customary to compost in the cultures of the gardeners. Rather than gathering in a common area, gardeners have built small huts on individual plots. They also tend not to reserve a space for a single purpose. A former gardener recalls, "They make little huts on their own plots, and a lot of people sleep there, take a little nap in the middle of gardening. Some of them would plant trees, so there would be a tree in the P-Patch, and some people would congregate around there. Those were great, serendipitous gathering spaces."

While the Thistle garden design is very utilitarian, the simple grid of plots has to mediate conflicts that arise from varied approaches to gardening. In this garden in particular, different styles of gardening exist within close proximity. For example, Korean and Hmong gardeners have contrasting ways of gardening. Korean gardens typically show a highly regulated structure, while the Hmong gardens lack any formal order. The difference can cause friction unless clear boundaries and edges are defined. Given the demand for gardening space, many of the Mien gardeners who cultivate to maximize their yield get frustrated by less productive gardens or by those who garden for fun. As one garden coordinator noted, "Other population groups don't work well in a Mien garden. Most of the Mien people garden to eat." Those who garden for recreation were often criticized by the more dedicated gardeners. As one former gardener recalled, "They would say, 'That's only two tomatoes! That's no good.' Some gardeners would get discouraged and quit." Accommodating the different gardening styles requires clear boundaries as well as cross-cultural knowledge and communication. A site coordinator with a multicultural background is therefore important.

5.6
A makeshift "hut" provides shelter and refuge in a garden used primarily for food production. Photograph by Jeffrey Hou, 2005.

FUNDING AND SUPPORT: EXTERNAL RESOURCES

Funding for the garden comes from the P-Patch Program, gardener fees, and other sources. Because P-Patch provides reduced fees for households that are low-income, many of the gardeners at Thistle pay significantly smaller fees than gardeners at other P-Patches. To fund some of the more expensive development projects, P-Patch seeks funds from city and private sources. A 1990 grant from Puget Consumer Cooperative (PCC), a local organic food retailer, allowed for the much-needed expansion of the water system and the garden plots. Further expansion of the gardening area and the water supply was supported through the Neighborhood Matching Fund. The garden recently received funding from the Community Development Block Grant to install a perimeter fence in the near future.

ORGANIZATION AND PARTICIPATION: A GARDEN MADE BY IMMIGRANTS

The Thistle garden is managed by the P-Patch Program through a Mien site coordinator, who also works as a bilingual agricultural instructor for the WSU King County Extension, a collaborative program between King County and Washington State University that focuses on agriculture, food and nutrition, and gardening, and promotes lifelong learning, self-sufficiency, and a livable environment through research-based education (WSU King County Extension 2006). In these two capaci-

5.7
A more elaborate hut anchors the corner of this plot. Photograph by Jeffrey Hou, 2006.

5.8
A temporary shelter sits on a temporary site. Photograph by Jeffrey Hou, 2006.

ties, the site coordinator not only handles the maintenance and logistics but also serves as an interpreter and instructs the gardeners on gardening techniques.

Most gardeners at Thistle come from other neighborhoods, including South Beacon Hill and unincorporated areas south of Seattle. Some come from far away because there are no other plots available. The diverse ethnic groups at the garden include gardeners from Korea, Vietnam, and different tribal people from Laos, including Mien, Hmong, and Khmu, with Mien gardeners making up the majority at the garden. On a typical day at Thistle, elderly gardeners work alongside moms with babies on their backs and children playing. Many of the immigrant gardeners were farmers in their home countries and have few other skills besides gardening and farming. Seniors and the underemployed often work in the garden all day. At least 50 percent of the gardeners are seniors, including several gardeners over the age of eighty. Only about 5 to 10 percent are younger gardeners, aged twenty to thirty-five.

PROGRAMS AND FUNCTIONS: A P-PATCH SERVING IMMIGRANT GARDENERS

If I don't have garden, I cannot do anything else, because that's all I know.
—A GARDENER AT THISTLE

Whereas many of the other community gardens have multiple programmatic elements, the Thistle P-Patch is primarily a place to garden, and gardeners observe P-Patch rules. However, there are some challenges in light of the different cultural practices at Thistle. For instance, while it is standard policy for each gardener to contribute eight volunteer hours each year toward the overall upkeep of the garden, the concept of volunteerism is alien to many of the Thistle gardeners—particularly the Hmong and Mien, who are not accustomed to engaging in collective labor outside their familial networks. The concept of a "work party" is foreign to them and has to be explained. As one Mien gardener describes nonfamily members, "We call them strangers or guests. We don't really ask them for help. We ask in the village only from cousins or someone you know for a long time." Cultural conflicts like this have resulted in some gardeners, mainly Hmong, leaving the P-Patch to garden in their home backyards. Fortunately, many gardeners do stay on and participate in work parties to clean up the site and rebuild the garden. Some gardeners even express enjoyment at participation in work parties and organized events. Many bring the whole family to the rebuild efforts, sharing food and working together with neighboring gardeners.

Because the garden serves primarily immigrant gardeners, helping immigrant gardeners adapt to local conditions has been an ongoing effort. Many gardeners have had to adjust to new climatic conditions and cultural settings. The climate in Seattle is too cold to grow some of the foods from their home countries. Many

5.9
A multilingual signboard greets visitors and neighbors to the Thistle P-Patch. Photograph by Jeffrey Hou, 2005.

of the gardeners are not able to read the labels of seed packages. Because communication with neighbors and city staff is often a problem, the multilingual site coordinator is essential not only to help the gardeners understand gardening techniques appropriate for the region but also to convey the P-Patch rules and to facilitate communication between gardeners speaking different languages.

CONTEXTUAL FACTORS AND CHALLENGES: CONFLICTS WITH NEIGHBORS

Situated in a relatively high-crime area and without any structural protection, the garden has been prone to theft and vandalism. Theft in particular has been a recurring problem for the gardeners at Thistle. Vegetables are often stolen, and individual storage sheds are sometimes broken into. As a residual space under a utility corridor, the site also attracts the dumping of garbage and even stolen vehicles. Addressing theft and vandalism through design has been a challenge.

Until recently, the garden was open on all sides. With public access a requirement and few resources for improvements, there is very little that the gardeners can do to prevent theft and vandalism in the garden. The constant problem of theft and vandalism often makes the gardeners feel powerless. "Lots of vandalism—and that's only thing I dislike. But I cannot win," said one gardener. Another gardener related, "One day somebody just walked through the fence and picked all the beans—nothing left. That's the only time that I felt so sad."

Several factors have led to tensions between the gardeners and the local community. Unlike Bradner or Magnuson, which encourage nongardeners and passersby to come onto the site, the Thistle P-Patch is designed solely to serve the gardening needs of those with plots. Because the site is fully utilized for gardening, storage materials such as wood chips often spill over the boundary of the site, causing complaints from neighbors. Parking is also an issue when gardeners and nearby residents compete for parking spaces. As a result, the immediate neighbors often complain about the garden. One former gardener speaks of the relations between the garden and the neighbors: "The residents along here hate the P-Patch. They hate it. [The neighbors] are not interested in gardening, and most of the gardeners are coming in from other areas."

Maintaining good relations with the neighbors is therefore critical to the continued use of the site as well as to receiving continued financial support from the city. To reduce tensions with the neighbors, the gardeners are constantly reminded by the staff to keep the garden clean and orderly: "This is city [property]. This is not any other garden or farm. If you don't help keep it clean, the neighbors write long letters to the city." Specifically, gardeners are reminded that they are "not farming in the countryside." Creating gathering places on the site and ongoing outreach may be necessary in the long term to enhance the collective ownership and management of the garden and the surrounding area. A sense of broader, collective ownership of the garden is needed for crime watches and theft and vandalism prevention to be effective. The building of the perimeter fence has addressed the problem of the lack of a defined edge and has created better control of public access and circulation. However, the problems are not likely to go away entirely through physical design alone.

SPECIAL LESSON: SERVING IMMIGRANT GARDENERS IN MULTIPLE WAYS

The Thistle P-Patch provides important economic, nutritional, cultural, and psychological benefits for its primarily immigrant and refugee gardeners. Economically, the garden allows immigrants and refugees to grow their own food in the face of limited income. The economic importance of the garden is reflected in the intensive use of the garden. Some families even consolidate their plots in order to maximize space. One former gardener reflected on her experience of gardening at

5.10
The adjacent neighborhood overlooks the sprawling garden. Photograph by Nathan Brightbill, 2006.

5.11
A newly installed perimeter fence helps define the boundary and identity of the garden. Photograph by Leslie Gia Clark, 2007.

Thistle: "They use every inch of land. The footpaths can barely fit my foot between the different plots. They're maximizing the production and really use it. . . . Time is limited, so everyone is focused on gardening when they are there. They will lose their plants if they don't work in the garden."

With vegetables from the garden, the families go to the store only to buy things that they cannot grow. The garden therefore provides a primary source of food for the gardeners. Some of the vegetables grown at the garden are not available in stores but are important to the cultures and diets of the gardeners. The freshness of vegetables from the garden is also something the gardeners appreciate.

Besides its economic and nutritional importance, the garden also provides important psychological and therapeutic benefits for immigrant and refugee gardeners. Having grown up helping their parents on farms, many gardeners express their enjoyment of simply working in the garden. To them, the garden reminds them of home. "I love to garden because I love to see plants grow," said one gardener. "I always come and watch my plants grow. I enjoy it. It always makes me feel happy," said another. The therapeutic aspect of the garden was vividly expressed by one gardener: "When I'm here in my garden, I don't feel sad or anything. I just keep doing whatever I feel I'm supposed to do. And I forget all my pain, and sadness, and other things. I don't really have time to think about it. . . . If I get to go out, I want to go to my garden. When I keep working like this, no pain. When I go home, I have lots of pain." Similarly, another gardener explained that the garden served as a form of therapy, stating, "When I have to see doctors or see my counselors, after that I say, 'Oh, I'm going to my garden!'"

In addition to the individual benefits it bestows, and despite the lack of a formal common space, the garden provides a place for gardeners to socialize and to connect with friends and others. One gardener expresses the joy of seeing and meeting with people at the garden: "I like to see my friends. And enjoying talking and seeing many kinds of people." Another mentions, "Here I see Hmong, Korean, Laos, and many other people, and lots of my friends, and lots of Mien people. I feel so great and happy." Less experienced gardeners also benefit from the social interactions involved in learning about gardening techniques. One gardener compares the P-Patch with her garden at home: "This is more fun because I get to see other people, and we work together and talk together, and we can exchange knowledge about planting." The garden has provided positive experiences not only to immigrant and refugee gardeners but also to those who are native to Seattle. One former gardener recalls, "People would bring food out there, and we'd sit under the tree in the shade. And we'd have this sticky sweet rice, just all kinds of goodies. . . . And the women were so friendly and so kind. . . . I ended up coming out quite a bit. I learned so much from them, and we could hardly communicate."

SPECIAL LESSON: COMMUNITY CHANGE ON THE HORIZON

As a community garden in an urban setting, the Thistle P-Patch garden is also faced with the uncertainty of change as the result of development. Despite persistent pockets of crime and poverty, Rainier Valley and the area surrounding the garden have improved over time. While the area is often perceived negatively by the rest of the city, the crime rate has dropped significantly in recent years. The area is again attracting home buyers and a resurgence of big-box retail stores and private investments. A number of affordable housing developments are underway, including

Rainier Vista, a HOPE VI public housing redevelopment that is replacing 481 low-income homes with 850 mixed-income residences (Snel 1999).

Along with current retail and housing developments, a new light rail line connecting the area with downtown and the rest of the region is likely to bring further growth. There are hopes of economic revitalization as well as fear of gentrification and displacement. A public fund of fifty million dollars was set up in 1999 to help offset some of the effects of the light-rail construction. The fund is being administered by the community for mitigation, transit-oriented development, community development, and job training, with the main goal being to avoid gentrification and displacement. Physical changes in the garden are not imminent since, as a utility easement, the site is off-limits to development. However, the changes in property values and the demographics of the area are likely to have an impact on the future of the garden, as the low-income immigrant residents may seek more affordable housing elsewhere. Furthermore, rising incomes among the immigrant families will also have an impact on the economic importance of the garden to the gardeners and on their involvement with and dependence upon the garden.

6

Danny Woo International District Community Garden

LOCATION: 620 South Main Street, Seattle

ESTABLISHED: 1975

CONSTRUCTED/REBUILT: 1975 to present

DESIGNER(S): Dan Rounds (1980 plan); Leslie Morishita (toolshed); UW Neighborhood Design/Build Studio (multiple elements)

MANAGED BY: Inter*Im Community Development Association

OTHER PARTNERS: Seattle Department of Parks and Recreation; Wilderness Inner-City Leadership Development (WILD); AmeriCorps; The Service Board; United Way; Youth Volunteer Corps; Voluntary Organization of Community Enterprise (VOICE); City Year; Community Action Partnerships (CAP); and the Friends of Danny Woo Community Garden

SITE OWNERSHIP(S): Wilma and Teresa Woo; Seattle Department of Parks and Recreation; Seattle Department of Transportation (street right-of-way)

LEASE/OWNERSHIP TERMS: private agreement; agreement with Seattle Department of Parks and Recreation

SIZE: 1.5 acres

NUMBER OF PLOTS: approximately 100

NEIGHBORHOOD STATISTICS: International District. Population 2,083, with median household income of $13,057. Ethnic/racial composition: 56% Asian; 15% white; 15% black; 6% multiracial; 5% Hispanic/Latino; 1% American Indian/Alaska native; 1% Native Hawaiian/Pacific Islander; 1% other (*Seattle Post-Intelligencer* 2006)

TOUR OF DANNY WOO COMMUNITY GARDEN

Sandwiched between the Interstate 5 and downtown apartment buildings, the Danny Woo International District Community Garden, together with the adjacent Kobe Terrace Park, forms one of the largest open spaces in downtown Seattle. A series of terraces, supported by railroad ties, provide flat areas for gardening. The hillside, once covered by blackberry brambles and trash, is now covered by a wide variety of Asian vegetables—bok choy, winter melon, shiso (beefsteak plants), garlic chives, chrysanthemum greens, beans, watercress, mustard greens, and garlic—that are cultivated by mostly elderly Asian residents. Cherry, plum, Asian pear, and apple trees add variety and flavor to the densely cultivated garden plots.

As a garden that serves predominantly immigrant Asian populations, the design of the garden reflects the cultural heritage of the community. The street frontage and steps up into the garden have been enhanced with an Asian-inspired gateway and other features. The steps lead up to a central area with a toolshed and a barbeque pit that serves as the social center of the garden. A series of kiosks and decks provide seating spaces for gardeners and visitors. With views of Elliott Bay, the Olympic Mountains, the Port of Seattle, the Mariner and Seahawk stadiums,

6.1
Urban context in the International District: the Danny Woo Community Garden is tucked between Interstate 5 and downtown apartment buildings. Map by Nathan Brightbill, with data from City of Seattle.

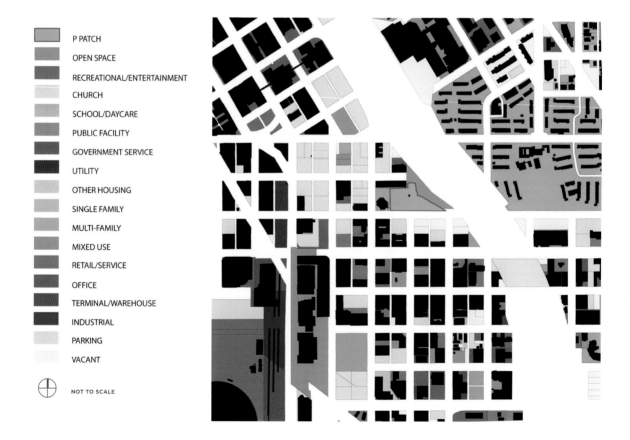

P PATCH

OPEN SPACE

RECREATIONAL/ENTERTAINMENT

CHURCH

SCHOOL/DAYCARE

PUBLIC FACILITY

GOVERNMENT SERVICE

UTILITY

OTHER HOUSING

SINGLE FAMILY

MULTI-FAMILY

MIXED USE

RETAIL/SERVICE

OFFICE

TERMINAL/WAREHOUSE

INDUSTRIAL

PARKING

VACANT

NOT TO SCALE

and the surrounding neighborhoods, the garden attracts not only gardeners but also nearby residents and sometimes tourists. As public access is required for Parks Department properties, the garden is open to and frequented by visitors year-round.

BACKGROUND AND HISTORY: REBUILDING AN INNER-CITY COMMUNITY

Situated on a hill overlooking the Japantown section of the International District, the Danny Woo Community Garden is both a symbol and an everyday embodiment of efforts to rebuild the historic ethnic community. The International District is one of Seattle's most historically significant neighborhoods. Settled by successive waves of immigrants since the nineteenth century, it has since served as a uniquely multiethnic neighborhood with predominantly Chinese, Japanese, Filipino, and, more recently, Southeast Asian residents. Throughout much of the twentieth century, the community prospered while enduring the tragic loss of Japanese businesses and residents as a result of internment during World War II. After the war,

6.2
Site plan of Danny Woo Community Garden, with the adjacent Kobe Terrace Park to the Northeast. Drawing by Nathan Brightbill.

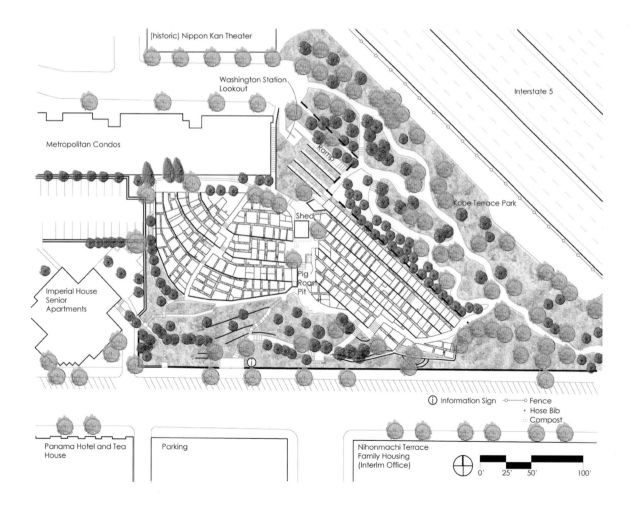

6.3
Danny Woo Community Garden provides an urban refuge for residents living in downtown apartments. Photograph by Jeffrey Hou, 2006.

many residents began moving to the suburbs, leaving behind a primarily low-income, elderly population. This population lived mainly in small apartments and single-occupancy hotels, with few places to exercise or socialize.

The 1.5-acre garden, the largest in the downtown area, was built in the midst of a community struggle in the early 1970s. The blighted condition of the historic neighborhood and threats of a stadium development brought together a group of pan-ethnic activists with the goal of protecting the community and providing affordable housing and services to the area's disadvantaged low-income and elderly residents. The idea of building a community garden emerged as a way to meet the desire of the elderly residents to stay physically active (Santos 2002). In 1975, a local businessman and restaurant owner, Danny Woo, agreed to allow activists to turn his vacant land adjacent to the freeway into a community garden. Initially offered as a short-term arrangement, the family never requested the land back. As a result, the garden became a lasting legacy of Danny Woo and was renamed "Danny Woo International District Community Garden" in his honor.

Managed by the Inter*Im Community Development Association (ICDA), a community organization that emerged from the struggle in the 1970s, the garden initially included forty plots. In 1980, the site expanded onto adjacent Kobe Terrace Park. The use of park property for a community garden was the first of its kind in Seattle. The Parks Department board was initially concerned that this would set a dangerous precedent (Santos 2002). This addition allowed for 100 plots to be available and has continued to be an integral part of the garden ever since.

DESIGN PROCESS AND IMPLEMENTATION: "A WORK IN PROGRESS"

The garden is a source of pride for the community because it was built by the community—we did that!
—A site coordinator

In its thirty years of operation, the Danny Woo Community Garden has undergone many changes and continues to evolve. At first, using railroad ties donated by the Burlington Northern Railroad Company, gardeners and volunteers started shaping the site, cutting terraces into the hillside, building makeshift retaining walls, and establishing staircases and paths. Starting in 1989, the garden design began to formalize and address issues of identity and orientation through the involvement of the Neighborhood Design/Build Studio at the University of Washington, led by Professor Steve Badanes. Working with residents, students and faculty designed and installed a series of important improvements, including a toolshed, an entrance gateway, a pig roasting pit, vegetable washing areas, kiosks, compost bins, accessible garden terraces, and garden paths.

Since then the Neighborhood Design/Build Studio has had a continuing presence in the garden. The design/build process for making the series of improvements involves a unique co-learning and collaborative process between the students and faculty, gardeners, and garden organizers. At planning meetings, the gardeners, garden manager, and ICDA staff first identify the garden's needs. Then, led by faculty, the students facilitate a collaborative process to develop a design and present it to the garden manager and gardeners.

As a continually evolving place, future changes and improvements to the garden have already been envisioned. Currently, there are plans to increase the number of plots by using additional park land, to create ornamental gardens and more seating

areas, and to enhance physical and visual connections within the garden and to the neighborhood. Other ideas for improvements include new storage areas, serviceable toilets, and a common work space. In 2005, a master plan process was initiated between Chinese-speaking gardeners and bilingual students from the University of Washington. Some initial suggestions brought forward by gardeners include improving the definition of the garden space through better edging and wider paths.

Neighborhood changes also suggest new opportunities for the garden and its evolution. For instance, a new affordable apartment building was completed across the street from the garden in 2006. Developed by ICDA, the building is expected to bring more users to the garden. Also, a Green Street Project on an adjacent street, linking the garden and the Chinatown area of the International District, is being planned to improve pedestrian and visual connections between the garden and the rest of the neighborhood. The project has been a result of collaboration between faculty and students at University of Washington and ICDA, along with other community partners. These improvements are part of a continuing effort to serve and improve the broader community in the district, the goal that led to the building of the garden in the first place.

6.4
(opposite, upper left)
The design of the toolshed reflects the cultural background of the gardeners. Photograph by Jeffrey Hou, 2006.

6.5
(opposite, upper right)
The staircase leading into the garden was one of the first design/build elements built on-site by students from the University of Washington. Photograph by Jeffrey Hou, 2006.

6.6
(opposite, lower left)
The arbor and pig-roast pit serves as the gathering space for gardeners and visitors. Photograph by Jeffrey Hou, 2006.

6.7
(opposite, lower right)
Garden terraces were designed to provide better access for elderly gardeners. Photograph by Jeffrey Hou, 2006.

6.8
The Danny Woo Community Garden provides an important amenity to a growing community; affordable housing apartments were recently constructed across the street. Photograph by Jeffrey Hou, 2006.

FUNDING AND SUPPORT: COMMUNITY ENTREPRENEURISM

The ICDA pays for all of the Danny Woo Community Garden's operation and maintenance costs as well as the property tax of the site. Funding comes from sources such as parking (ICDA operates a park-n-ride facility under Interstate 5), developer's fees, and impact capital. Additional capital improvements and programs are supported through a variety of grants and outside sources, including the Department of Neighborhoods matching funds, corporate donations, Washington Insurance Council, Washington State Department of Natural Resources, Seattle Housing Authority, private foundations such as the South Downtown Foundation and Norman Archibald Foundation, local construction companies, private individuals, and in-kind support from volunteer organizations and local schools. The expansion in 1980 was supported with a grant from HUD's Neighborhood Self-Help Development grant program, the only non-housing application out of 700 submissions (Santos 2002). Funding for materials used in the design/build studios is raised through grants and donations by ICDA. The in-kind contribution of labor by the UW Neighborhood Design/Build Studio also helped leverage funding, especially from the city's Neighborhood Matching Funds.

ORGANIZATION AND PARTICIPATION: SERVING A SPECIAL POPULATION

As one of the few non-P-Patch, independent community gardens in Seattle, the Danny Woo Community Garden has a different approach to its operation and maintenance compared with the P-Patch gardens. The nonprofit ICDA has been a key player in the creation and management of the Danny Woo Community Garden. Established in 1969 as the International District Improvement Association by the district's business community and changed to Inter*Im Community Development Association in 1975 as a 501(c)(3), ICDA has been an important community organization in the district, with a mission to maintain the affordability, livability, and character of the neighborhood. Its work includes community development planning and advocacy, affordable housing development, public policy advocacy, and support for other community-based organizations. The ICDA arranged with the Woo family to pay the site's property taxes in exchange of use of the land. The garden is also supported by the Friends of Danny Woo Community Garden and an advisory group that includes a network of individuals, professionals, businesses, and other community organizations. From the very beginning, P-Patch staff have also provided technical assistance.

Whereas the P-Patch gardens are open to any resident in Seattle, the Danny Woo Community Garden is intended to serve a specific population—the International District's low-income elderly. Priority for plot assignments at Danny Woo is given to residents who are low-income (making 30 percent less than the median income), sixty-five and older, and living within the bounds of the International District. Those on the waiting list receive a score based on these three criteria. Currently, the average age of the gardeners is sixty-seven, and 80 percent are non-English speakers. Many of the gardeners live in nearby apartments. Garden plot contracts are renewed on a yearly basis during the spring registration, with preference given to returning elderly gardeners and low-income residents. In some cases, gardeners have renewed their plots for many years, including one couple that has gardened here since the garden first opened in 1975. Once getting their plots, most gardeners do not want to give them up—even when it becomes difficult for the more elderly gardeners to make it to the gardens. Half a dozen gardeners are now in their eighties. In recent years, the garden has started to accept younger gardeners if vacant plots are available in order to create a more mixed population and also to acquire additional help in maintaining the garden.

The garden is overseen by a garden manager hired by the ICDA, who has the responsibility of assisting gardeners, coordinating volunteers, balancing individual and public use of the space, managing language and cultural nuances, and obtaining the resources to improve the gardens. Over its thirty-year existence, the Danny Woo Community Garden has been fortunate to have had several effective and committed garden managers who continue to build the garden socially and physically on a daily basis. However, given the demanding work, retaining a highly effective garden manager is also a struggle for the Danny Woo Community Garden as an independently operated community garden whose financial resources are limited.

In addition to the gardeners and ICDA staff, many volunteers have contributed to the building and maintenance of the garden. A long history of volunteerism at the garden has helped to build the garden not only as a physical place but also as a broad community of residents, activists, and volunteers. Because many of the gardeners are elderly, volunteers assist with the physically demanding construction and maintenance needs, such as building the retaining walls, pruning fruit trees, and maintaining the common areas. Other volunteers assist at meetings by translating the various languages spoken in the garden. Volunteers also lead tours and educational workshops in order to share the resources and history of the gardens with the larger community. One or two volunteering events a month are regularly held at the garden. Volunteers are recruited from nearby universities, the AmeriCorps program, groups such as the Alaska Cannery Workers Association, and other volunteer organizations such as City Year and the Service Board.

To celebrate these efforts, the garden continues to have an annual pig roast, an event that was initially started in 1975 to celebrate the completion of the garden. The annual event brings together gardeners, activists, volunteers, and other neighborhood residents and reminds them of the shared history of the garden and of the community's struggle back in the 1960s and 1970s.

6.9
The annual pig roast at the
Danny Woo Community
Garden brings activists
and gardeners together
to celebrate the history of
the garden and community
activism. Photograph by
Leslie Gia Clark, 2007.

PROGRAM AND FUNCTIONS: LOCAL FOOD SECURITY, EDUCATION, AND HABITAT

While the primary function of the site is to provide a place for elderly residents to garden, this activity is linked to other goals, such as socialization, exercise, nutrition, and community building. Gardeners can grow foods appropriate to their culture while also saving on their household bills. At the same time, the garden provides opportunities for the elderly to get out of their small apartments in order to exercise and socialize. The site also serves as a venue for a wide variety of educational and volunteering activities for local residents as well as outside organizations and individuals.

In 2005, educational workshops were organized for the gardeners in order to engage the elderly gardeners during the off-season. At the workshops, gardeners shared their gardening wisdom and learned about sustainable practices such as using organic fertilizers and not using pesticides. In addition, tours and workshops are organized either by the garden or by outside groups that simply use the garden as an educational setting to conduct their program.

As a green open space located in a dense urban area, the Danny Woo Community Garden provides an additional function as habitat for urban wildlife. Seeds, berries, and insects attract a great variety of birds. Bird sightings range from hummingbirds to woodpeckers to hawks (Stratten 2001). For this reason, the garden serves as a venue for community events and educational programs related to urban sustainability. For example, workshops have been held in coordination with local college programs and organizations to promote and demonstrate benign tree pruning. There have also been composting workshops for youth groups, cub scout groups, and environmental justice organizations.

CONTEXTUAL FACTORS AND CHALLENGES: ADDRESSING THE PRESENCE OF ILLICIT ACTIVITIES

There are times when there are too many homeless. So I'll check if my friends or others are out working there, or else I won't go out.
—AN ELDERLY GARDENER

As one of few publicly accessible open spaces in downtown Seattle, the Danny Woo Community Garden has its share of problems and challenges. One of the main challenges is the presence of illicit activities, such as drug use and prostitution, in the adjacent Kobe Terrace Park, which tends to spill over into the garden's gathering spaces. The presence of transient individuals and vandalism and the occasional stealing of vegetables often make the elderly gardeners uncomfortable if not apprehensive. One gardener who lives nearby said that she will not come out at night because she is scared of the drug dealers and transients. She states, "If there is no one else in the garden, then I quickly finish what I'm doing and go home." Because of language and cultural barriers, most gardeners do not report crimes to the police. The problem and perception of crime prevent the garden and the park from being fully utilized and enjoyed by the residents and gardeners.

Because the garden occupies city property and therefore must be maintained as a public space, it is virtually impossible to secure the garden against many of these activities. The isolated location of the garden between the interstate freeway, a poorly used urban park, and tall apartment buildings also makes it difficult for police surveillance. Preventing the illicit activities from taking over the garden is a daily struggle for gardeners and for the garden manager in particular. There have been different ideas about how to address the issue of safety among those involved in the garden. One approach was to put gates at entrances and eliminate some of the entrances to control circulation into the garden. Others argue that the place could be made more public and attract more users to deter the illicit activities. A designer involved in the garden said, "The idea is that if you can make it a little bit more open to the public, it could be a little safer."

The concern for safety is only part of a more fundamental struggle to balance the use of the garden as a place for gardeners and a place for the public. For example, an excessive degree of ownership among some gardeners (especially those who have been around for five, ten, or even twenty years) has made the garden look more private than public. To discourage theft, some gardeners have barricaded their plots to prevent access, thereby making the garden less publicly accessible. Working with the gardeners to maintain the garden for the benefit of low-income seniors and to provide an open space for the community at large, a central mission of the garden, becomes a daily balancing act—especially for the garden manager.

SPECIAL LESSON: FULFILLING THE MULTIPLE NEEDS OF ELDERLY IMMIGRANT GARDENERS

All my friends together talked about wanting to garden. Most of us had never done it before. So I thought I'd like to try it myself, too. And we didn't have much of a chance to exercise. So we thought it would be good to take advantage of the health benefit. And also growing our own organic vegetables.

—AN ELDERLY TAIWANESE GARDENER

Begun as a simple act to provide a place for elders to engage in physical activities, the Danny Woo Community Garden provides multiple benefits to its target users. By growing food for household consumption, low-income seniors living on shoestring budgets and government subsidies can focus their income on other needs. The garden also provides a way to continue the seniors' agricultural heritage and cultural traditions. One Korean gardener we interviewed, who grew up on a farm, was pleased to be able to pick up farming again. But not all elders knew how to garden—especially those coming from densely developed Asian cities, such as Taipei. At the Danny Woo Community Garden, they were able to learn from other gardeners who have more knowledge and experience. One elderly Taiwanese gardener in her eighties said, "Not until I reached age seventy-eight have I learned how to plant vegetables. Coming here and watching people do it, I find it very fun."

For many of the gardeners, coming to the garden is one of the few opportunities they have to go outside their small apartment units and meet with other people. The slope of the site can be challenging. But many elderly gardeners use it as an opportunity for exercise. One Korean gardener said that gardening is a good hobby and great for health, stating, "I like it because the seniors do nothing. They like to come and take care of their vegetables. It's one kind of hobby. Main thing, seniors' health, y'know?" Similarly, an elderly Taiwanese gardener mentioned the therapeutic and health aspects of gardening: "When we visit our plants daily, and they grow a little each day, then we are very happy. And the fresh air is very good for us too. And exercising."

While the garden has been popular among immigrant elders, language and cultural barriers are ongoing challenges for the management of the garden. Currently, at least six different languages and dialects are spoken at the garden, including Korean, Mandarin Chinese, Cantonese, Toisan, Ho'lo Taiwanese, and Japanese. Although the garden manager can rely on bilingual volunteers for translating at regular meetings and large events, daily communication presents a challenge between

6.10
Many elderly gardeners in the Danny Woo Community Garden check on their plots as part of their daily routine. Photograph by Leslie Gia Clark, 2007.

non-English-speaking elderly gardeners, the garden manager, and predominantly white volunteers. For instance, communication about the dangers of pesticides and the potential to use more environmentally and healthy alternatives is complicated by language barriers. Unlike the city's P-Patch program, which bans the use of pesticides, a quarter of the gardeners at Danny Woo still use pesticides. Many of the gardeners cannot read the warning labels of pesticides. Resolving occasional frictions between gardeners who speak different languages is also a problem. Multiple translations are often needed, with help from bilingual and multilingual gardeners.

SPECIAL LESSON: COMMUNITY DESIGN/BUILD

The continuing involvement of UW's Neighborhood Design/Build Studio contributes to another unique feature of the garden and provides lessons for conducting design/build projects in an immigrant community. In the short ten-week quarter, students develop designs, refine them, and construct the structures. This short time period has its own challenges, as students may have to start construction before getting full approval for their design. Additionally, there are language and cultural barriers that slow down the communication process. Luckily, these barriers can be overcome when the student volunteers include first- or second-generation Asian Americans who are bilingual.

Because elements have to be designed and built by students while also being easily maintained, simple construction techniques are used at the garden. But the effects are rich and complex. The architectural style and the system of wood framing

6.11
A recent design/build addition transforms a problem spot in the garden into a welcoming gathering area.
Photograph by Leslie Gia Clark, 2007.

recall traditional Chinese and Japanese wooden architecture. The structures provide order and identity to the makeshift garden. They also create places for gardeners and visitors to sit and spend time in the garden. The style is particularly effective in providing cultural familiarity to the elderly immigrants who are adjusting to conditions in their new homes in Seattle (Hou 2005). Although each project is developed independently, the long-term relationship has led to a design vocabulary and quality of construction that shapes the garden's identity.

The incremental nature of the design/build process also gives the garden a unique character that is distinct from typical urban parks. Rather than a master plan or a totalizing design, continued adaptation is possible and necessary. The student work provides an "infrastructure" by focusing on public areas and perennial gardens and allowing gardeners and volunteers to do the rest. Despite the presence of the numerous structures of similar motifs, the garden still looks ad hoc, active and alive with the seasonal changes of vegetation and people and the weathering of structures and landscape.

7

Bradner Gardens Park

LOCATION: 29th Avenue South and South Grant Street, Seattle

ESTABLISHED: 1987 (as the Mt. Baker P-Patch)

CONSTRUCTED/REBUILT: master plan completed 1995; construction 1998–2003

DESIGNER(S): Barker Landscape Architects (master plan); Scott Carr of SHED Architects (community building); UW Neighborhood Design/Build Studio (pavilion, bridge, trellis, arbors)

MANAGED BY: Friends of Bradner Gardens Park (not a 501[c][3]), in cooperation with Seattle Department of Parks and Recreation

OTHER PARTNERS: King County Master Gardener program; Seattle P-Patch Program; Seattle Tilth Association; Master Urban Gardeners; Seattle Department of Parks and Recreation, Washington Native Plant Society

SITE OWNERSHIP(S): Seattle Department of Parks and Recreation

LEASE/OWNERSHIP TERMS: Memorandum of Agreement (MOA) with Seattle Department of Parks and Recreation

SIZE: 1.6 acres

NUMBER OF PLOTS: 43 (each 10 x 20 feet; Seattle Department of Neighborhoods 2008)

NEIGHBORHOOD STATISTICS: Mount Baker neighborhood. Population 5,717, with median household income of $53,447. Ethnic/racial composition: 52% white; 23% black; 18% Asian; 2% Latino; 1% American Indian/Alaska Native; 4% other (*Seattle Post-Intelligencer* 2006)

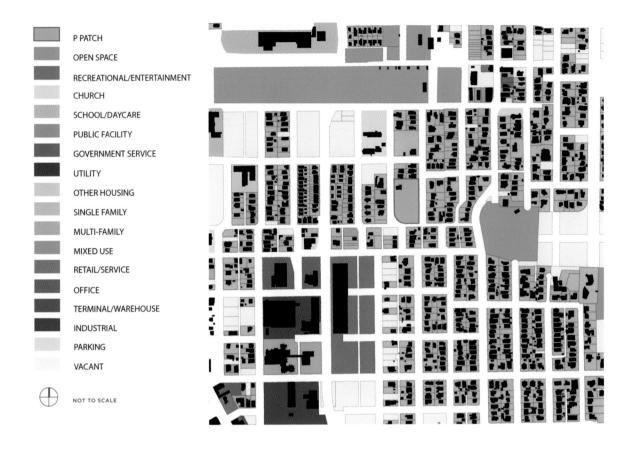

	P PATCH
	OPEN SPACE
	RECREATIONAL/ENTERTAINMENT
	CHURCH
	SCHOOL/DAYCARE
	PUBLIC FACILITY
	GOVERNMENT SERVICE
	UTILITY
	OTHER HOUSING
	SINGLE FAMILY
	MULTI-FAMILY
	MIXED USE
	RETAIL/SERVICE
	OFFICE
	TERMINAL/WAREHOUSE
	INDUSTRIAL
	PARKING
	VACANT

NOT TO SCALE

TOUR OF BRADNER GARDENS PARK

Located in the ethnically diverse but changing Mount Baker neighborhood of central Seattle, Bradner Gardens Park, formerly the Mt. Baker P-Patch, is a visually striking composition of art, vegetation, and community engagement. Surrounded by artful objects and buildings, the community garden is only one aspect of this nontraditional neighborhood park. The vibrancy of sculpture and vegetation in the garden's foreground are complemented by spectacular views of the downtown skyline.

Accessible on three sides by streets, the park is entered through a series of arbors constructed out of steel, wood, and quarry spalls. The periphery includes colorful plantings in a sequence of themed demonstration gardens, with plant identification tags to aid the curious passerby. At the top and southeastern corner entrance, stone steps and open lawn capture the best view of the downtown skyline and provide a popular area for events and community gathering. The center of the park is marked by a prominent, leaf-shaped pavilion that also serves as the main gathering place.

Located next to the pavilion are more demonstration gardens, including a children's garden and a demonstration urban organic food garden. To both sides are

7.1
Bradner Gardens
Park is located in
the predominantly
residential Mount Baker
neighborhood in southeast
Seattle. Map by Nathan
Brightbill, with data from
City of Seattle.

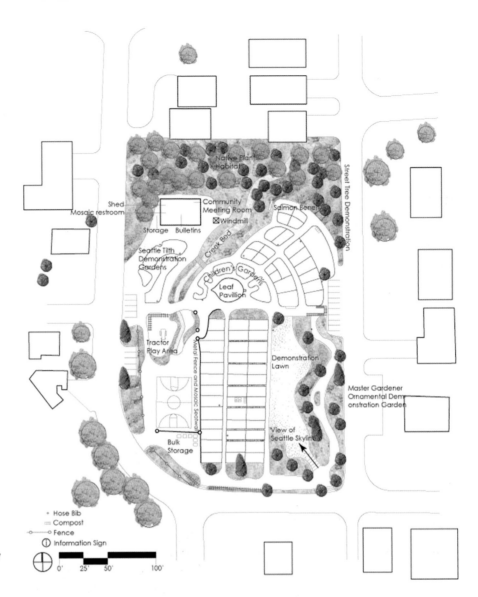

Labels within the image:
Native Plant Habitat
Shed
Mosaic restroom
Community Meeting Room
Windmill
Salmon Bench
Street Tree Demonstration
Storage Bulletins
Creek Bed
Seattle Tilth Demonstration Gardens
Children's Gardens
Leaf Pavillion
Tractor Play Area
Metal Fence and Mosaic Seatwall
Demonstration Lawn
Master Gardener Ornamental Demonstration Garden
View of Seattle Skyline
Bulk Storage

• Hose Bib
⊐⊐ Compost
○──○ Fence
ⓘ Information Sign

0' 25' 50' 100'

7.2
Site plan of Bradner
Gardens Park. Drawing by
Nathan Brightbill.

community garden plots that express a range of gardening practices and personalities. At the northern end is the award-winning community building that serves as toolshed, meeting room, and restroom. Incorporating elements of a previous structure as well as new construction, the building received the 2003 Honor Award by the Seattle chapter of the American Institute of Architects. A surprising gem is the mosaic restroom, which has been rated as one of the best public restrooms in Seattle by a local newspaper. That the bathroom has not been the victim of vandalism has been attributed to appreciation of the public bathroom and its beauty. Beyond the building and along the northern edge of the site, a native plant and wildlife habitat serves as a buffer between the park and the neighboring houses.

To the west, the vegetable plots give way to other uses. A children's play area is thematically linked to the garden with an antique tractor and farm equipment. In

7.3
At one time the "million-dollar" view of downtown Seattle from the park had almost tempted the city into selling the property. Photograph by Jeffrey Hou, 2006.

similar fashion, a basketball court is framed by a fence that is decorated with old gardening tools. Beyond the basketball court is a delivery area for compost, mulch, and other elements that help make the garden function.

BACKGROUND AND HISTORY: "PROTECT OUR PARK"

The unique character of Bradner Garden Park is a telling reminder of the enthusiasm and participation that went into making this community space. The 1.6-acre site was one of nineteen sites purchased by the city in 1971 for neighborhood parks.

However, instead of being developed as a park, the land was used for a middle school annex until 1975. From 1975 to 1983, the four portable school buildings on the site served the Central Youth and Family Service (Friends of Bradner Gardens Park 2006). In 1987, the P-Patch Program established a community garden in an open area of the site in order to provide gardening spaces for local residents—particularly for Mien immigrants from Laos that lived in the community and elsewhere. In the meantime, the P-Patch also served as an ad-hoc community gathering place.

Local activism to establish a permanent park began in earnest in 1994 when residents learned about the city's plan to capitalize on the site's stunning views by selling the site for market-rate housing development. Community residents formed the Friends of Bradner Gardens Park and lobbied the city council and officials to keep the park site and the P-Patch gardens. While organizing supporters, signing petitions, and lobbying officials, the group also applied for and received a $4,500 award from the Small and Simple Projects Fund from the Department of Neighborhoods in 1995 to hire a landscape architect to develop a master plan for the park.

Unable to persuade the city to keep the site, the Friends then developed a more extensive strategy to protect park land in the city's increasingly development-prone neighborhoods. Working with other open-space activists around the city, they drafted a "Protect Our Parks" initiative , which set forth a policy to address park distribution prior to selling park sites. With 24,000 signatures collected, the initiative was approved by the city council and became a city ordinance. The ordinance, which states that "land designated for park use cannot be sold, traded, or used for nonpark use unless it is replaced with like kind in the same neighborhood," has been a victory not only for Bradner Gardens Park but also for other neighborhood park sites in Seattle facing similar threats. Under the ordinance, the usage for Bradner Gardens Park was approved in 1997.

DESIGN PROCESS AND IMPLEMENTATION: CREATIVE RESPONSES TO FULFILL MULTIPLE FUNCTIONS

This park is a place that looks very different from what the Parks Department would do.

—A GARDENER AT BRADNER

With some garden plots already in use, the overall master plan for the park was developed by Barker Landscape Architects, working with gardeners and local activists in on-site design workshops and public meetings conducted through the Parks Department and the P-Patch Program. Through translation, the Mien gardeners were also involved in the meetings. Between 1998 and 2003, different areas of the park were developed incrementally through a concerted effort by neighborhood activists, residents, and professionals. The design expanded the number of community garden plots from thirty-nine to sixty-one plots. A series of community spaces

7.4
The Park Master Plan was produced with support from the Neighborhood Matching Fund. Courtesy of Barker Landscape Architects.

were defined, including the central pavilion, a path system compliant with the Americans with Disabilities Act (ADA), an open lawn area, a playground, and a basketball court.

One of the most important aspects of Bradner Gardens Park is demonstrating how urban community gardens can co-exist successfully with other program ele-

7.5
Details of the entry arbor that give the garden a visual identity and deem the place a "pesticide-free zone." Photograph by Vanessa Lee, 2005.

ments in a park-like setting, and particularly how this can be done through design and planning.

Commenting on the competing uses on the site, community activist and site coordinator Joyce Moty notes that "Bradner is an unusual public space in that it defies conventional thinking in park design" (1999). The multiple uses of the park were defined in the master-plan process, with each key partner set to develop and maintain a part of the site. The designer used the metaphor of a plant to organize the different program elements on the site, with "a central stem representing the old garden that terminated in a pavilion and central gathering place and then all of the gardens from there kind of radiated out like a plant growing." To emphasize inclusiveness, the entire garden is designed for ADA access. Even the small footbridge over the pond is designed to allow two wheelchairs to pass at a time.

A partnership that aided in creating the unique character of the site is the collaboration with University of Washington Neighborhood Design/Build Studio. Through this partnership, students and faculty worked with residents and artists to develop various structures in the park. Led by Steve Badanes, the partnership began in 1998 when the Friends group received a grant from the Department of Neighborhoods and the Puget Sound Urban Resources Partnership for park improvements, including the arbor entrances. In 2000, the studio was invited back to build the central pavilion and an additional arbor entrance. Participation of UW studio enables the community to obtain the Neighborhood Matching Fund.

Over the span of five years, individual elements of the park were designed and built with the help of UW's Neighborhood Design/Build Studio and other architects. These include the leaf-shaped central pavilion, the entry arbors, a pond, and the community building with a toolshed and public restroom. By using easy-to-find materials and relatively simple construction processes, it has been easy for new elements to follow the language started in the earlier improvements (Palleroni 2004). As one gardener mentioned, "If there is something I don't like, I will think of something and try to do it myself." The strong design framework maintains the flexibility to incorporate art and later interventions. As architecture professor Steve Badanes acknowledges, "If the community changes, then the project has to change."

In addition to the design/build projects, Bradner Garden Park is also notable for an abundance of artworks created by local artists and volunteers. They range from decorated hose bibs and pillars to scarecrows made from found objects to a

7.6
(above)
Located in the center of the park, the leaf-shaped pavilion serves as the focal point and gathering place for gardeners and park users. Photograph by Leslie Gia Clark, 2007.

7.7
(far left)
Art spigot. Utilities transformed into inspiring found art via a garden-wide contest can be seen throughout the park. Photograph by Vanessa Lee, 2005.

7.8
Voted as one of the best in the city, the public restroom features a mosaic mural designed by local artists. Photograph by Leslie Gia Clark, 2007.

7.9
A recycled windmill
reinforces the park's
identity as an urban farm.
Photograph by Vanessa
Lee, 2005.

"salmon bench" that depicts the life cycle of salmon. Rather than opting for a chain link fence around the basketball court, volunteers designed and built an artful fence made from heavy wires and decorated with rusty farming tools to reflect the urban agricultural theme. Under the fence are large concrete blocks decorated with tile-and-glass mosaics made by local youth. The inclusion of sculpture and art throughout the garden reflects the participation of many artists—ceramic artists, fiber artists, and sculptors—who have connections to a larger network of artists interested in providing garden art.

FUNDING AND SUPPORT: LEVERAGING

As a park property, Bradner Gardens Park is regularly maintained by the Seattle Department of Parks and Recreation. However, additional funding has been necessary to realize the park master plan. In order to raise money, the Friends of Bradner, which is not a 501(c)(3), has arranged for a fiscal relationship with the Mt. Baker Community Club to enable fundraising. Altogether, about $450,000 in total has been raised through grants and private foundations. Based on the initial master plan, the community building was made possible through funding from the Pro Parks Levy ($222,696), along with additional funding of $162,465 from other public and private sources (Seattle Parks and Recreation 2006). To restore the basketball court and develop the play area, funding came from the North Rainier plan and King County Youth Sports Facility Grant. The Washington State Department of Natural Resources provided $3,500 for trees in the park. Some of these grants leveraged additional funding. For example, a total of $209,500 was awarded from the Neighborhood Matching Fund when the money was plentiful, which leveraged an additional $1,100,000 for the park (Diers 2004). To meet the match requirement for the Neighborhood Matching Fund, the organizers count the work conducted by volunteers and the University of Washington faculty and students.

ORGANIZATION AND PARTICIPATION: PARTNERSHIPS

Bradner Gardens Park is managed by a volunteer committee. The garden's main organizational body is the Friends of Bradner Gardens Park, which meets monthly and consists of two people from each of the garden's partner organizations—the WSU King County Extension Master Gardener program, the Seattle P-Patch Program, the Seattle Tilth Association, the Master Urban Gardeners, and the

Washington Native Plant Society. Each of these groups is actively engaged in the site's development and programming. For example, the Washington Native Plant Society has developed the habitat area that borders the northern edge of the site and includes native plants. The Seattle Tilth Association maintains a demonstration children's garden and urban food garden. The Master Gardeners maintain the themed gardens along the border of the park and provide occasional workshops. The Seattle P-Patch Program provides support for individual garden plots.

Besides the key partners, several other organizations have expanded the possibilities within the garden. For instance, King Conservation District assisted with the development of native-plant wildlife habitat and provided the plants and planting plan that includes over forty native trees and shrubs in the region. Seattle Public Utilities and the Department of Parks and Recreation provided additional native plants. An organization called Tree Stewards worked with Seattle City Light and the City Arborist's office to select trees for display as part of the Seattle Millennium Woods Legacy celebration in 2000.

Volunteers play an important role in improving the park and strengthening the coalition and community support. Much of the construction occurred on volunteer workdays. Altogether, 40,000 volunteer hours were logged in the first four years, including volunteers from churches, employee groups, schools, and other non-profit organizations. To get the garden built, the organizers held work parties every two weekends a month, with volunteers working in three-hour shifts. While some people have stayed involved from the beginning, others leave and new volunteers join the effort. Volunteerism is sustained through regular events and activities that include work parties, a July Fourth potluck picnic, a Halloween costume cider-press party, garden concerts, plant sales, and workshops. These activities help support the continued improvements and maintenance of the park. They also help build a greater support network beyond the park and neighborhood. The different groups—such as the Seattle Tilth, the Native Plant Society, and the Master Gardeners—also bring their own volunteers and resources to the site. For example, Seattle Tilth has supervised school groups that provide community service.

While volunteers play an important role, managing volunteers and building community also place a big burden on the site coordinator, itself a volunteer position. The core group of people that do most of the work are also volunteers. Although the gardeners also put in some volunteer hours, they are not necessarily from the community. "Their community may be something else, like their church or their work or their neighborhood block," said one informant. Communication with multiple cultural groups also presents a challenge. Because of language barriers, the non-English-speaking gardeners may miss out on information disseminated during meetings and via e-mail. Although most gardeners have e-mail, not all are proficient in English.

7.10
Seattle Tilth children's garden. Photograph by Arielle Farina Clark, 2005.

7.11
The Master Gardener's demonstration garden surrounds the park with ornamental plantings. Photograph by Arielle Farina Clark, 2005.

PROGRAMS AND FUNCTIONS: A GARDEN FOR LEARNING

We see ourselves as being a learning resource to the community and the
city at large.
—A SITE COORDINATOR

P-Patch

The park includes sixty-one community garden plots. These ten-by-twenty-foot
plots are held to the standards and regulations of the P-Patch Program. Gardeners
agree to abide by P-Patch rules and to pay a nominal fee that helps pay for water
and upkeep. The plots are kept in their original location so as not to disturb the gardening activities while other park elements are being developed. As a result, rather
than being pushed to one side of the site, the P-Patch gardens occupy a prominent
location within the park and give the park a unique identity. The location allows the
garden to be fully integrated into the park design.

Education, Demonstration, and Theme Gardens

Because the park engages organizational partners with missions related to gardening
and environmental education, it serves as a showcase and experimental ground for
a variety of activities. Informational and interpretative signs can be found throughout the site that engage visitors in understanding the gardening practices and
techniques. Seattle Tilth sponsors demonstrations on topics such as drip irrigation
systems, cover cropping, mulching, and composting (Friends of Bradner Gardens
Park 2006). Master Gardeners hold free gardening workshops that address topics
such as plant propagation, drip irrigation, soil building and testing, winter gardening, summer harvesting and food preservation, and making art pavers and pots
(Moty 2003). Under guidance of volunteers from Master Gardeners, P-Patch, and
Seattle Tilth, children grow vegetables organically as a generous gift to local food
banks (Friends of Bradner Gardens Park 2006). In addition to garden-related workshops, there is a mosaic workshop that doubles as a fundraising event.

Besides organized workshops and tours, learning occurs through demonstration
gardens and overall site plantings. Throughout the site there are more than fifty
varieties of ornamental street trees recommended for small spaces and under utility lines. Along the periphery of the garden, there are themed gardens developed by
master gardeners to illustrate alternative options for small urban residential yards,
including areas to show butterfly and hummingbird habitat, winter interest gardens, sensory gardens, shade gardens, native plant gardens, fragrance gardens, and
dry gardens. Each garden features a selection of plants that demonstrate the right
species for specific contexts, low maintenance, and a variety of irrigation systems.
These gardens provide examples for lectures, demonstrations, and workshops.

The park also includes a Seattle Tilth demonstration garden that showcases edible plants, herbs, and plants that attract beneficial insects. Because Bradner Gardens Park is one of Seattle's first pesticide-free parks, there are also opportunities to observe sustainable gardening practices.

On an everyday basis, the gardens are places of learning. Gardeners teach each other about gardening and improving soils. For example, gardeners learn about composting and the cycle of gardening through volunteer work supervised by the site coordinator. Gardeners from other gardens around the city also frequently visit the park. Other visitors have come from as far as the Midwest and Asia. One gardener commented, "Most people go to Bradner to see what's been done. So it triggered more interest and excitement to create more P-Patches." Gardeners are encouraged to talk about the history of the garden and park if a visitor asks for information. For the Mien gardeners, the plots at Bradner provide a place to continue their cultural traditions. One gardener noted, "I learned about [gardening] from my mother in my country when I was small. Right now we keep the seeds year by year. We did that in Laos." Gardeners also interact cross-culturally. One gardener commented that "multicultural interactions can happen even with the language barriers."

7.12
The basketball court became an unexpected partner by bringing more users to the park and allowing kids to play while their parents garden in the P-Patch. Photograph by Jeffrey Hou, 2006.

Functioning as Garden and Park

To an outsider, it would seem that an active recreational element such as a basketball court would be at odds with a gardening area. An errant ball could potentially destroy crops, and the meditative state that many gardeners seek could be destroyed by the noise of a game. However, this is not the case at Bradner, where creative solutions play an important role in resolving the conflicting uses of the park. Despite initial hesitation by some gardeners, those in favor of including the basketball court have won over. The conflicts between the basketball court and the adjacent garden plots were resolved by putting up an artful fence between the two.

Other elements, such as the central pavilion, make the park a place of gathering and function as an outdoor community center (Moty 1999). The mixture of uses proves to be beneficial to both the park and the garden. In the case of the basketball court, the presence of basketball players apparently helps the gardeners to feel safer when gardening alone. The recreational elements also occupy and entertain gardeners' children so that they can work in their plots. Preschoolers come to play in the park on a daily basis.

The mixed-use aspect of the park supports a variety of community events, including concerts and an annual Halloween party, July Fourth picnic, and New Year's Eve burn. As described by one gardener, the New Year's Eve burn encourages people to "bring along either their wishes for the New Year or their regrets from the last year, and write it on a piece of paper or wood and throw it into the burn barrel." There has even been a wedding in the garden. Page Crutcher, one of the designers with Barker Landscape Architects, argues, "What is really successful about a community garden in an urban area is that it brings a new activity to these park spaces. Sometimes people don't feel safe in parks. Here is one [example]: you get these regular people who are neighbors, who have much more investment in a project."

She also notes that the mixture gives the park a unique identity; "Parks always have a certain amount of lawn, playfields, basketball, that kind of things. But this really is a kind of unique expression of the neighborhood." One of the site coordinators says, "More people came to the garden than just the gardeners."

CONTEXTUAL FACTORS AND CHALLENGES: GENTRIFICATION AND NEIGHBORHOOD CHANGE

Karen Daubert, executive director of the Seattle Parks Foundation, described Bradner as "a model of models" for the country (Easton 2005). However, the success of Bradner Gardens Park also brings a new set of challenges. Like other areas in the city that have experienced improvements, rising housing prices have led to gentrification of the neighborhood. The neighborhood in Mount Baker, once perceived of as problematic, dangerous, and having lower land values, has become an attractive place because of its proximity to downtown and the prized view of the downtown skyline. As result of rising property values, many residents have been priced out of the neighborhood. For example, Laotian immigrants no longer live in the neighborhood. Currently, only six of the original Laotian families continue to have garden plots—mainly because they want to sustain their personal attachment and friendships with other gardeners. However, one gardener is considering leaving because of the time and distance it takes to come to the site. Given the trend for the continued rise in property values, retaining the diversity of gardeners and residents and making the garden an inclusive place presents a challenge to sites such as Bradner.

SPECIAL LESSON: GREEN BUILDING PRACTICES

Since the opening of the park, ongoing partnerships with local agencies and professionals have made Bradner a showcase of green and sustainable design. The

7.13
The community building/ toolshed reused an existing on-site structure and incorporates solar panels and a rainwater collection system on its rooftop. Photograph by Jeffrey Hou, 2006.

community building, designed by SHED Architects, successfully incorporates most of the preexisting concrete-block storage room and restroom. The new community meeting room features a natural-gas fireplace and day lighting. The building has a new roof system that incorporates a grid-connected photovoltaic system generating a net surplus of power. The project involved collaboration between Seattle City Light, the Department of Parks and Recreation, Friends of Bradner Gardens Park, SHED Architects, and the Washington State University Northwest Solar Center. It uses a variety of sustainable materials, including renewable agricultural fiber by-product, recycled plastics, and engineered and sustainably harvested lumber. The gabion pillars that support the arbors were built from heavy wire mesh and filled with quarry spall and sometimes rusty gardening tools. Lawns are made of Ecoturf, a mix of various turf-type lawn grasses and water-wise broadleaf perennials, forming a dense lawn-type planting (Seattle Public Utilities 2006). The community building also includes a roof-water-collection system with three water storage tanks for use by gardeners. A thirty-three-foot-tall vintage windmill recirculates site runoff collected in the seasonal pond to the dry streambed next to the children's play area and back into the pond. Finally, the spigots have signs that read, "Water wisely." These design elements not only introduce sustainable design practice to the park but also serve as demonstration and learning tools for the gardeners and visitors. With assistance and support from various agencies, the implementation of these elements also brings much-needed resources to help realize the park's master plan.

8

Marra Farm

LOCATION: Fourth Avenue South and South Director Street, Seattle

ESTABLISHED: 1997 (restoration efforts and P-Patch); 1998 (gardens created by coalition of groups)

CONSTRUCTED/REBUILT: continued development since 1997; master planning effort 2006/7

DESIGNER(S): Jones and Jones Architects and Landscape Architects (initial master plan); University of Washington architecture students Mark Haizlip and Greg Squires (shed design and build); Department of Parks and Recreation, supported by University of Washington landscape architecture student Eric Higbee (master planning effort); J. A. Brennan Associates (preliminary draft master plan; posted on Parks Department Web site)

MANAGED BY: Marra Farm Coalition (MFC) and Seattle Department of Parks and Recreation

PARTNERS IN COALITION: Lettuce Link; Seattle Youth Garden Works; Mien Community Garden members, including WSU King County Extension garden staff members; South Park Area Redevelopment Committee; IMAPAL Foundation; community members

SITE OWNERSHIP(S): Seattle Department of Parks and Recreation

LEASE/OWNERSHIP TERMS: agreement with Seattle Department of Parks and Recreation

SIZE: 8.7-acre site, of which half is farm with four gardens; P-Patch on 5,600 square feet (Seattle Department of Neighborhoods 2005); Lettuce Link on .75 acre; Mien Community Garden on .75 acre (Seattle Department of Parks and Recreation 2006); and Seattle Youth Garden Works on 1 acre (SYGW 2005)

NUMBER OF PLOTS: 28 P-Patch plots (Seattle Department of Neighborhoods 2005), plus gardens for Lettuce Link, Seattle Youth Garden Works, Mien Community Garden

NEIGHBORHOOD STATISTICS: South Park neighborhood. Population 3,717, with median household income of $30,917. Ethnic/racial composition: 37% Hispanic/ Latino; 34% white; 14% Asian; 7% black; 5% multiracial; 2% American Indian; and 1% Native Hawaiian/ Pacific Islander (*Seattle Post-Intelligencer* 2006)

TOUR OF MARRA FARM

Nestled in an industrial and residential district between two major highways, one of the last two agricultural lands in Seattle is being revitalized as a local food producer and a destination for learning and recreation. Although relatively unassuming from the outside, this farm offers many programs and experiences. From the gravel parking area at the northeast corner of the farm, an open meadow provides a threshold.

8.1
Marra Farm is tucked into a residential and industrial area of the South Park neighborhood, between two highways. Map by Nathan Brightbill, with data from City of Seattle.

P PATCH

OPEN SPACE

RECREATIONAL/ENTERTAINI

CHURCH

SCHOOL/DAYCARE

PUBLIC FACILITY

GOVERNMENT SERVICE

UTILITY

OTHER HOUSING

SINGLE FAMILY

MULTI-FAMILY

MIXED USE

RETAIL/SERVICE

OFFICE

TERMINAL/WAREHOUSE

INDUSTRIAL

PARKING

VACANT

NOT TO SCALE

A kiosk with a "welcome" sign greets the visitor and provides a space for informal notices and descriptions of the farm's gardens, which are also marked by post-and-wire fences and entry gates. To the left, one sees a native plant restoration area with an interpretive sign. Behind this, a densely vegetated slope extends south and separates the farm from the vacant elevated field that completes this park property. Looking ahead, a cluster of cottonwood trees serves as an informal gathering space, with informal seating clustered within. To either side, one sees the garden structures of storage sheds (one with a Marra Farm mural) and sinks mounted in a wood frame table. While exploring the flat farm site, one finds picnic tables, kiosks, storage sheds, compost areas, interpretive signs and kiosks, and a portable toilet.

Various cues indicate the programs occurring on the farm. To the right of the parking area, a large multilingual sign, symbolic gate structure, and seating area denotes the Mien Community Garden, whose gardeners cultivate a three-quarter-acre area using traditional methods, such as a network of upright twigs to support plants. The Seattle Youth Garden Works area is marked by a colorful sign spanning a tall torii-style wood-frame gateway, and a similarly bright sign marks a side

8.2
Existing site plan of Marra Farm with P-Patch garden denoted by central gridded area. Drawing by Nathan Brightbill.

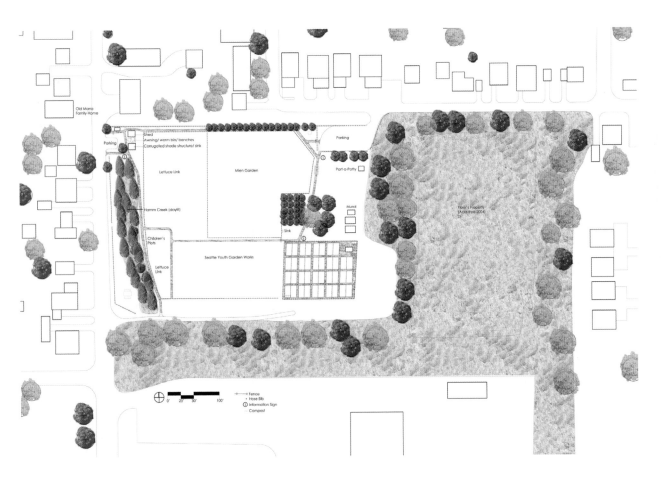

8.3
A simple gate welcomes visitors to the Mien Community Garden in Marra Fram. Photograph by Vanessa Lee, 2006.

8.4
The Lost Fork of Hamm Creek flows along the west edge of the Farm. Photograph by Julie Johnson, 2007.

gate. Beyond are long rows of mounded planting beds, with produce grown at the scale appropriate for marketing. Some rows are planted, while others lie fallow. The P-Patch garden to the south, identified with a bilingual sign over its gate, has a fine-grained quality, as gardeners have filled their ten-by-twenty-foot plots with an array of vegetables, herbs, and flowers. At the northwest corner lie the one-acre Lettuce Link garden, with rows for food bank produce, and the circular beds of the children's garden, as well as an outdoor classroom space and storage shed. The Lost Fork of Hamm Creek flows gently along the farm's western side. Recently daylighted and restored, the creek provides not only an area for animal habitat—including salmon—but also an attraction for local children and their families. On the other side of the creek, a split-rail fence runs along Fourth Avenue South, with single-family homes facing the farm. The southern edge of the farm is bounded visually and physically by a tall berm, with blackberry and other shrubs, intermixed with a row of poplar trees. Only a small portion of the neighboring recycling facility is visible, although its sounds, along with those of passing airplanes and the adjacent highway, intrude upon the calm of this verdant landscape.

BACKGROUND AND HISTORY: A FARM RECLAIMED

Marra Farm was once home to the Marra family, who had bought it from Joe Desimone in 1920 and farmed the land into the 1970s (Seattle 2007; Solid Ground 2007). King County purchased the land with the condition that it remain farmland, and in 1997 restoration work by neighbors and a VISTA volunteer got underway (SYGW 2005; Solid Ground 2007). Starting in 1998, other groups and programs joined in and organized as the Marra Farm Coalition (MFC) (Solid Ground 2007; SYGW 2005). In 2004, ownership of the farm and adjacent open space was transferred from King County to the City of Seattle Department of Parks and Recreation (Seattle Department of Parks and Recreation 2006).

Marra Farm occupies half of an 8.7-acre open space in the ethnically diverse South Park neighborhood. South Park contains the highest percentage of Latinos in the city, and households below the poverty line comprise more than 12.5 percent—as compared to 8.4 percent for Seattle (Higbee 2006). The neighborhood has only two small grocery stores and no supermarket, so the farm's productive family and giving gardens (where produce is donated to local food banks) play a meaningful role in providing fresh produce (Solid Ground 2007).

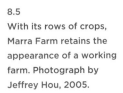

8.5
With its rows of crops, Marra Farm retains the appearance of a working farm. Photograph by Jeffrey Hou, 2005.

DESIGN PROCESS AND IMPLEMENTATION:
INCREMENTAL CHANGE

In 2000, the MFC asked Jones & Jones Architects and Landscape Architects to help create a master plan for the farm and creek restoration. Goals and desired elements were identified in response to a preliminary vision plan prepared by the firm to initiate discussion. Two alternatives were developed, from which MFC selected parts to create one master plan (Jones and Jones 2000). The involved groups and volunteers began developing the site, as grants and other funds and opportunities were secured. For instance, in 2003, officials from the King Conservation District hired Healing Hooves to bring eighty goats and fifteen sheep to clear the eastern side of the farm. After three days of eating blackberry thickets, grasses, ivy, and knotweed, the animals were moved, and volunteers grubbed out the remaining roots, covered the area with landscape fabric, and mulched (Alexander 2003).

In 2005, the MFC received a Seattle Pro Parks Levy grant to undertake a long-term development plan of the entire 8.7-acre site, as well as articulate a management plan and begin construction of some elements. The schedule identifies planning in 2005–2006, design in 2006, and construction in 2006–2007 (Seattle Department of Parks and Recreation 2006). The planning effort has been assisted by a University of Washington graduate student in landscape architecture, Eric Higbee, who focused his thesis on developing a farm master plan and engaged in community outreach to understand community goals and needs. The Parks Department managed this planning effort, solicited community ideas at community meetings, and postponed the summaries on its project Web site (Seattle Department of Parks and Recreation 2007a). The first meeting was held in conjunction with the farm's "Fall Fest" in October 2005, in which community ideas were sought via a questionnaire. The second meeting was held in late April 2006, with ten tents staffed by various agencies and MFC volunteers providing information on the farm: its history; the creek; and elements such as signs, paths, fences, composting toilets, playgrounds, and recreational facilities. Approximately 120 people came to this Saturday meeting, and Spanish, Vietnamese, and Mien translators were present to help convey ideas (Seattle Department of Parks and Recreation 2007b). The third meeting, in early June 2006, included various questions about potential changes to the farm for agriculture and recreation, particularly play oppor-

8.6
At the 2005 Marra Farm Fall Fest, landscape architecture thesis student Eric Higbee helped gather ideas for the farm's master planning process. Photograph by Vanessa Lee, 2005.

tunities for children (Seattle Department of Parks and Recreation 2007c). At the October 2006 Fall Fest, Parks Department staff and their consultant held an open house/meeting to provide information and answer questions about the long-range development plan, with supportive responses (Seattle Department of Parks and Recreation 2007d).

In addition to the planning of future elements, a garden element was developed through the efforts of two University of Washington architecture graduate students, Mark Haizlip and Greg Squires, who undertook a design/build thesis project. In 2005, their thesis included the design of a "community classroom" on the site, with the construction of a storage shed to support Lettuce Link's educational program. This effort served as a dual learning experience, as the thesis students engaged local children from Concord Elementary School in building the new shed (Haizlip and Squires 2005; AIA Seattle 2006). The project was supported with an internship offered through the College of Architecture and Urban Planning, fundraising by Lettuce Link, other donations, and volunteers (Haizlip and Squires 2005). Additionally, the other pieces of this space—an outdoor classroom and a cleaning/kitchen space—were created in 2006 through support of a Small and Simple Projects Fund and volunteers (Lettuce Link 2006).

FUNDING AND SUPPORT: DIVERSE SOURCES FOR MYRIAD IMPROVEMENTS

Marra Farm has benefited through support from foundations, the city, the county, federal programs, and the in-kind contributions of volunteers. As noted on its interpretive sign, the creek daylighting was undertaken by the IMAPAL Foundation, the King Conservation District, and a King County Parks Department work crew. A project coordinator was hired through a grant from the Puget Sound Urban Resources Partnership to work with all of the farm's gardening groups (Raymond 2000). A Community Development Block Grant enabled the installation of a large water meter, replacing the past use of a fire hydrant for water (Macdonald 2005). Lettuce Link's outdoor classroom and kitchen were realized with support from a City Department of Neighborhoods Small and Simple Projects Fund and volunteers (Lettuce Link 2006). The MFC has continued to secure support and grants for improvements and to foster greater community connections with the farm. A Race and Social Justice grant through Seattle's Department of Neighborhoods provided $11,091 for outreach to engage the neighborhood's Spanish-speaking community (Lettuce Link 2005). In September 2005, an award of $180,000 from the Seattle Pro Parks Levy Opportunity Fund was made for a community-based master plan, management plan, and construction of elements (Seattle Department of Parks and Recreation 2006).

Like other gardens, the MFC and its garden groups have partnered with other organizations and sought volunteers to make improvements. In 2004, an event held by the American Institute of Graphic Arts resulted in a new logo for the farm (Macdonald 2004b). The farm was included in an annual conference organized by the nonprofit Pomegranate Center titled "Community-Built Gathering Places" (Macdonald 2004a). The involvement of college students provides tangible benefits, as students volunteer for particular programs as well as envision and make improvements such as the Lettuce Link shed. Additionally, corporate and individual volunteers help to maintain the gardens.

ORGANIZATION AND PARTICIPATION: A COALITION OF INTERESTS

The Marra Farm Coalition is comprised of several gardening organizations, as well as the IMAPAL Foundation, the South Park Area Redevelopment Committee (SPARC), Master Gardeners/Master Soil Builders, and community members (Seattle Department of Parks and Recreation 2006). MFC community members include Fred Marra, whose family had farmed the land, and other neighbors. Participating gardening organizations include the Seattle Department of Neighborhoods' P-Patch Program, Lettuce Link, Seattle Youth Garden Works (SYGW), and the Mien Community Garden. Lettuce Link, a program of the nonprofit Solid Ground, is dedicated to urban agriculture and food security, and provides produce and seeds to area food banks. SYGW, run by the Church Council of Greater Seattle, serves local at-risk youth through a market garden educational and employment program. The Mien Community Garden, managed by a WSU King County Extension garden educator who is a member of the Mien community, uses traditional Mien agricultural practices.

The Marra Farm Coalition has defined its mission as being to "address community food security needs, provide a space for sustainable agriculture education, and engage community members" (Seattle Department of Parks and Recreation 2006). Over the years, there has been some change in the groups gardening at Marra Farm, with the most recent gardening group being the Mien Community Garden. Each group has a discrete focus and audience, yet the groups' collaboration has helped to bring mutual benefits and serve the MFC mission. The recent addition of programs by the Master Composters/Master Soil Builders at Marra Farm further supports this mission.

PROGRAMS AND FUNCTIONS: SERVING INDIVIDUALS AND TARGETED GROUPS

P-Patch

Marra Farm P-Patch includes twenty-eight plots for gardeners (Seattle Department of Neighborhoods 2005). The P-Patch's Web site description complements

8.7
The large east gateway to Seattle Youth Garden Works frames a view of the plots. Photograph by Jeffrey Hou, 2005.

8.8
The Lettuce Link shed designed and built by UW Architecture thesis students supports an outdoor classroom space. Photograph by Vanessa Lee, 2006.

the MFC mission, while identifying community benefits: "At Marra Farm people come to learn about organic produce cultivation, food-related issues, and environmental stewardship. . . . We work to cultivate the innate values of community gardening: friendships, community building, self-reliance, neighborhood open-space, environmental awareness, hunger relief, improved nutrition, recreation, gardening education, and therapeutic opportunities" (Seattle Department of Neighborhoods 2005).

Because of the desire for more community representation in the farms' activities, there have been outreach efforts to attract gardeners from the South Park neighborhood. The P-Patch Program was featured on a local Spanish-language radio station, with two gardeners and the radio host, also a gardener; two callers requested plots (Macdonald 2004a). With greater neighborhood participation, the garden includes Latino, Mien, and white gardeners.

8.9
A bilingual sign marks the entrance to the P-Patch garden. Photograph by Vanessa Lee, 2006.

Mien Community Garden

It's a lot [of] land; they can plant bean[s] here. Last year bean was in this corner; this year down here, next year maybe a bit in. . . . I tell them they have to do it good and it will last for long time.

—MIEN GARDENER

Started in 2003, the farm's three-quarter-acre Mien Community Garden engages members of the Mien community. Traditional Mien agricultural approaches are undertaken, and the produce serves the Mien community and is contributed to local food banks. A WSU King County Extension staff member who is Mien coordinates and works in this garden.

Lettuce Link

The MFC's mission of food security, education, and local engagement is central to the efforts of Lettuce Link. This program manages a giving garden at Marra Farm that in 2004 provided 13,000 pounds of organic produce (Lettuce Link 2005). This produce is donated to the local food bank, as well as to Women, Infants and Children (WIC) clients of a neighborhood health clinic, nearby Concord Elemen-

8.10
Supportive structures distinguish the Mien Community Garden plantings from the rest of Marra Farm. Photograph by Jeffrey Hou, 2005.

8.11
The circular forms of the children's garden enable easy access to individual students' plots. Photograph by Julie Johnson, 2007.

tary's students and families, and a shelter for women and children (Chansanchai 2005; Lettuce Link 2005). Lettuce Link's educational outreach has included nutrition classes for WIC Clients at the health clinic, a partnership with the Operation Frontline program for outdoor cooking classes at the garden, and an educational program with children from Concord Elementary School (Harper and Ferguson 2002).

As a K–5 school with close to 300 children, Concord Elementary has a diverse student body, the largest groups being Latino (60 percent) and Asian (17 percent). Approximately 89 percent of the school's children meet the requirements for free or reduced-cost lunches (Concord Elementary School 2005). Throughout the spring, children tend and study tiny individual plots in the children's garden, with a plan to host a salad bar for the school on two days in 2005 (Lettuce Link 2005). In 2004, fifty children from the school learned about nutrition and gardening at the Farm (Lettuce Link 2005), and more than 100 students participated in the expanded garden space in 2006 (Lettuce Link, 2006/2007).

The Lettuce Link garden also helps educate others who volunteer their time, as noted by a representative: "We have corporate volunteers who would never really be that interested in farming or organics or think twice about it. But they get their hands dirty, and they learn about it hands-on. And then they think about things differently....We also have interns and students who come work at the farm and learn about it."

Seattle Youth Garden Works

In 2000, Seattle Youth Garden Works (SYGW) established a market garden at Marra Farm to serve as an educational and employment program for local at-risk youth (SYGW 2005). The program receives funding from HUD, Washington State, and approximately thirty area foundations (Davis 2006). Starting small, the garden has grown to its current size of one acre, although a third of it is kept fallow each year for soil conservation and regeneration. Raised beds are tilled by hand using sustainable agricultural practices. Youth sell their produce at nearby farmers' markets and donate a portion to a local food bank. In addition to providing youth with gardening skills and employment, the program serves as science education that can help fulfill students' requirements for graduation (Davis 2006). Youth aged fourteen to eighteen apply to the program, and ten are selected for a crew that works together for two to three months. Three crews are assembled each year, spring, summer, and fall, with times set to work collectively. In 2005, approximately fifty applicants applied to be on one crew. Many of the youth are immigrants, primarily East African, but also Latino and Southeast Asian.

The program creates greater ties to others in the community and to the farm. A program representative observed, "I think it definitely gives you the opportunity to feel more connected, not only with each other, youths from different communities,

8.12
Pumpkins decorated at the Farm Fall Fest lie below a shed's mural. Photograph by Vanessa Lee, 2005.

but the community at large." This connection seems apparent, as the Marra Farm board of directors and volunteers include youths who have participated in the program (Davis 2006). Previous experiences at the Farm have also been noted by staff: "Sometimes we've hired people who've helped put salmon in the stream when they went to Concord as an elementary school kid. So some of the people in the neighborhood have deepened the connection of it being their space."

Gatherings and Public Events

Marra Farm also serves as a site for special events. While directing the efforts of local outreach through targeted programs and the Parks Department master-planning process, Marra Farm's gardens and identity as one of the last remaining agricultural lands in Seattle attract people from well beyond its neighborhood. For years, a "Fall Fest" at the farm has brought the farm to life with food, music, and other activities (Harper 2003). It is featured as a site for the annual King County Harvest Celebration Farm Tour (Hughes-Jelen 2002; WSU King County Extension 2007). Service projects attract corporate and other volunteers to the farm. The unique collaboration of program elements also attracts visits by other activists and nonprofit organizers. For instance, when the Community Food Security Coalition had its conference in Seattle, attendees visited the site (Harper and Ferguson 2002). In 2004, Marra Farm was part of the nonprofit Pomegranate Center's annual conference (Macdonald 2004a). The farm was visited in June 2005 as part of the AIA Seattle's annual Summer Solstice Procession (AIA Seattle 2006).

CONTEXTUAL FACTORS AND CHALLENGES: A GREEN ENCLAVE

Oh yeah, before I even had a spot over here, I used to come here and bring my kids and we used to just walk around where the water runs over there.
—A P-PATCH GARDENER

As a large open space, Marra Farm provides opportunities for gardeners to enjoy an escape from urban life in a neighborhood where open space is rare. Despite the four garden group plots on the farm, the currently used area of the site is not perceived as being overly active. When asked what is most enjoyable about gardening, a Marra

Farm gardener replied, "The quiet. It's very quiet down there. You hear birds. I like doing things with my hands. . . . It's sort of meditative and relaxing." Yet the farm's isolation also holds perceived and real challenges. One gardener recalled someone being concerned about gardening at night, as she saw people who intimidated her.

Nevertheless, this quiet respite from the city attracts a variety of visitors. A garden representative describes community use as including P-Patch gardeners, children playing, and people coming at lunchtime (Chansanchai 2005). Some people come to the farm while walking their dogs. The value of the farm as a local destination is well-stated by a South Park youth who participated in SYGW: "I think that South Park's Marra Farm is a great contribution to the South Park kids and adults of the neighborhood. Some examples of this is when kids or adults want to take a walk, and get away from the streets. This is one of the only places to go. It is also a very beautiful place to go. You can look at different kinds of produce, and sit and relax under the trees" (Fremont Public Association 2005).

Some conflicts arise between the gardening and the recreational uses of the space. For instance, some people walking their dogs at the farm do not attend to their pets' impacts. Garden fences and gates have become a necessity to protect the vulnerable plants from trampling. Despite the presence of fences to keep dogs out, one gardener noted, "I don't like how a lot of people are just bringing dogs around and they walk through your garden, and you know, they don't respect what you [have] got over there; because I know they can walk their dogs, but they cannot just let them run wild, because there are vegetables and plants growing. We eat those plants."

Vandalism and theft of produce concern some of the gardeners. Some confusion about taking produce may be attributed to a time when Lettuce Link representatives invited local residents into the garden to harvest food for their own consumption. That approach has been discontinued. A representative notes the need for more local involvement: "What we're trying to do at Marra is to invite the community down so that they can take ownership of it—all generations take ownership of it—so that there's hopefully less of a tendency that people destroy it, because it's now their friend who did that."

SPECIAL LESSON: THE URBAN FARM EXPERIENCE AND OPPORTUNITY

A once-neglected open space, Marra Farm has been revitalized as a source of organic produce, education, and recreation through the efforts of myriad groups and individuals. Greater local involvement is recognized and sought as key to its long-term success. The Parks Department planning process and implementation of the master plan hold potential for engaging the local community such that the farm may serve as a robust and valued community open space for learning and recreation. The future of the 4.5-acre farm and its adjacent site as a city park is already being informed by a new name. In early 2007, the Parks Department renamed the 8.7-acre property "Marra-Desimone Park," announcing in the city's press release, "The new park name hails from the farm's history. In 1920, Italian immigrants Carmine and Maria Marra purchased the farm [from] Joe Desimone of Pike Place Market fame" (Seattle Department of Neighborhoods 2007).

While more recreational and garden facilities are part of the master plan, the farm's current uses are valued. A local resident who gardens in the P-Patch notes the educational and personal values of the garden, stating, "I bring my son and daughter so they learn about how to grow their own vegetables, because I want them to know it's not just that you go to the store and buy it." This gardener also offered insights on what urban gardening offers those who cannot afford to own land, in describing what makes Marra Farm special: "It's special for me because I can grow vegetables; I can come here any time that I want, and no one can tell me not to be here. And I'm not the owner of this piece of land, but I know I can make decisions in this space because it's been assigned to me, and I can grow vegetables, and I can come here everyday."

Marra Farm provides a unique context within Seattle to retain and express an agricultural presence that is both historic and contemporary. While serving the nutritional needs of the local community through individual and collective efforts, it affords learning and recreational opportunities that will be enhanced and likely attract more local and regional users as the master plan becomes realized.

8.13
As traces of their gardeners, a row of chairs is shaded by P-Patch corn. Photograph by Vanessa Lee, 2005.

9

Magnuson Community Garden

LOCATION: within Warren G. Magnuson Park, 7400 Sand Point Way NE, Seattle

ESTABLISHED: 1977 (Sand Point P-Patch established); 2001 (relocated to Magnuson)

CONSTRUCTED/REBUILT: 2001–4

DESIGNER(S): Barker Landscape Architects (master plan and construction drawings)

MANAGED BY: Magnuson Community Garden (nonprofit organization); Department of Neighborhoods P-Patch program; Department of Parks and Recreation

OTHER PARTNERS: Magnuson Community Garden's native plant nursery involves Department of Parks and Recreations; Magnuson Environmental Stewardship Alliance; Native Plant Society; EarthCorps; U.S. Geological Survey (USGS)

SITE OWNERSHIP(S): Seattle Department of Parks and Recreation

LEASE/OWNERSHIP TERMS: Memorandum of Agreement (MOA) with Seattle Department of Parks and Recreation

SIZE: 4 acres

NUMBER OF PLOTS: 140 as completed (each 10 x 10 or 10 x 20 feet) (Seattle Department of Neighborhoods 2005)

NEIGHBORHOOD STATISTICS: Sand Point neighborhood. Population 7,781, with median household income of $65,530. Ethnic/racial composition: 82% white; 10% Asian; 3% Hispanic/Latino; 2% black (*Seattle Post-Intelligencer* 2006)

P PATCH

OPEN SPACE

RECREATIONAL/ENTERTAINMENT

CHURCH

SCHOOL/DAYCARE

PUBLIC FACILITY

GOVERNMENT SERVICE

UTILITY

OTHER HOUSING

SINGLE FAMILY

MULTI-FAMILY

MIXED USE

RETAIL/SERVICE

OFFICE

TERMINAL/WAREHOUSE

INDUSTRIAL

PARKING

VACANT

✳ SITE OF OLD P-PATCH GARDEN

⊕ NOT TO SCALE

9.1

Magnuson Community Garden lies at the end of one of Warren G. Magnuson Park's entry roads; the former Sand Point P-Patch was sited across from the park, in the dark brown parcel owned by the Children's Hospital. Map by Nathan Brightbill, with data from City of Seattle.

TOUR OF MAGNUSON COMMUNITY GARDEN

The Magnuson Community Garden is located in the 350-acre Warren G. Magnuson Park, the second largest park in Seattle (Seattle Department of Parks and Recreation 2006a). When driving into the park, the entry sign lists "community garden" as one of many recreational features. As one passes the park's Community Activity Center, views of an orchard, ponds, and a terraced amphitheater, crowned by an arbor and colorful plantings, suggest a unique kind of garden to be explored. Unlike the orthogonal grid found in many community gardens, Magnuson's organic pattern of paths and P-Patch plots flows easily along a gentle slope. As one gardener described it, "It's an ambling garden."

The winding paths converge on a slightly raised central gathering area that is marked by an artistic sundial and informal seating along the perimeter. This area provides an opportunity for prospect, as one can see much of the P-Patch, the adjacent park playground and dog off-leash area, and other areas of the park from this location. Sounds from these adjacent uses, as well as an abundance of bird song, fill the air. A native plant border frames the P-Patch to the south and east, separating it from a drive and the playground and dog off-leash area. To the north, and tucked

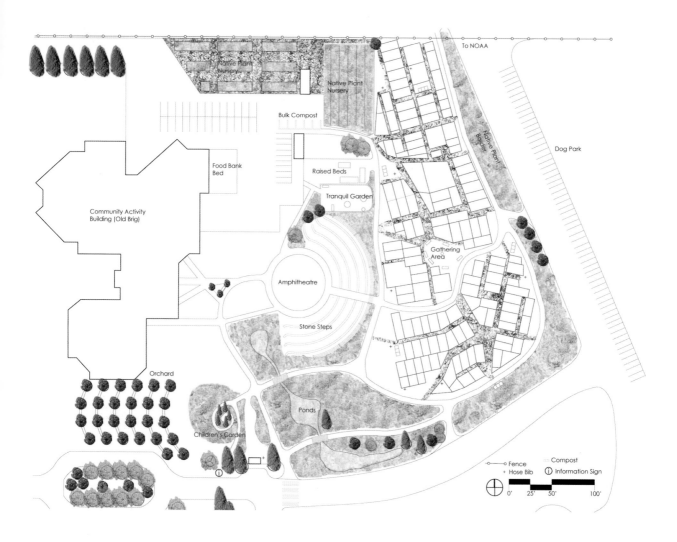

Labels within the drawing:

Native Plant Nursery

Native Plant Nursery

To NOAA

Bulk Compost

Native Plant Border

Dog Park

Food Bank Bed

Raised Beds

Tranquil Garden

Community Activity Building (Old Brig)

Gathering Area

Amphitheatre

Stone Steps

Orchard

Ponds

Children's Garden

Fence
Hose Bib

Compost
Information Sign

0'   25'   50'   100'

into the sloping terrain, is the tranquil garden—a patio area edged by plantings and a trellis-like fence to create a sense of enclosure. A small fountain provides a visual and auditory focus for the space. Accessible, raised P-Patch planting beds, a shed, a compost area, a native plant nursery, and a small parking area lie north of this garden. One hundred and forty plots, each roughly ten by ten or ten by twenty feet, are arranged in groups. The plots are bounded by an array of materials, including stones, wood, concrete blocks, bricks, and plastic lumber. This eclectic quality is further expressed with elements such as a birdhouse and arbor structures rising above the vegetation and a miniature "stroll garden" of diverse container plantings bordered by an engraved, rustic wooden bench.

As a four-acre garden within a vast urban park, this community garden serves varied garden constituents and a larger public. Not only is it a place for individuals to garden, it is also an inviting place to stroll and enjoy programmed activities for young and old.

9.2
Located alongside the park's Community Activity Center and north of the playground, diverse gardens and features comprise the Community Garden. Drawing by Nathan Brightbill.

9.3
From the children's garden mound one can view the pond area, the amphitheatre, and the arbor with the P-Patch beyond, as well as the parking area and shed. Photograph by Leslie Gia Clark, 2007.

9.4
Former aircraft hangars in the background recall the site's previous use as a Navy airfield. Photograph by Jeffrey Hou, 2005

BACKGROUND AND HISTORY: A GARDEN WITHIN A PARK

A convergence of events and efforts brought the Magnuson Community Garden into existence. Its genesis was the termination of the Sand Point P-Patch that had been gardened on land leased from the Children's Hospital and Regional Medical Center since 1977 (Magnuson Community Garden 2006a). Looking for a new site, the gardeners identified an opportunity to relocate the garden within Magnuson Park, a proposed new city park to be located on a former naval airfield just a block from the P-Patch. With its extensive waterfront, historic buildings, and open space, the mayor-appointed Blue Ribbon Committee envisioned Magnuson Park as "A Great Urban Park" containing "recreation, the arts, environmental protection and restoration, education, and residential" uses (Seattle Department of Parks and Recreation 2006b). The gardeners successfully lobbied for a P-Patch to be included

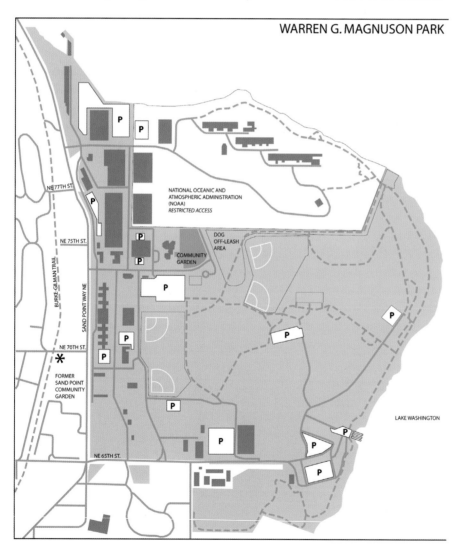

WARREN G. MAGNUSON PARK

9.5
The Magnuson Community Garden is a small area within Warren G. Magnuson Park, located near several former Naval buildings. Map by Nathan Brightbill and Leslie Gia Clark, adapted from Seattle Department of Parks and Recreation, Enterprise Division.

9.6
Looking across the
amphitheater, the gray
Community Activity
Center is visible, with the
View Ridge neighborhood
beyond. Photograph by
Jeffrey Hou, 2005

in the park's programming. In 1999, the city council adopted the Magnuson Park Concept Design with its resolution concluding, "Council encourages early implementation of the proposed community garden/Pea patch" (Magnuson Community Garden 2006b; City of Seattle Legislative Information Service 2008).

With this support, a group of gardeners met in late 1999 to organize efforts toward acquiring Neighborhood Matching Funds that would enable initial planning and design. Gardeners and other organizations formed the Magnuson Community Garden Coalition (later becoming a nonprofit called the Magnuson Community Garden). The multiple stakeholders shared a vision "to promote urban ecology, environmental stewardship, beautification of the park, education, and healthy food gardening" (Magnuson Community Garden 2006c). In autumn 2001, Sand Point P-Patch gardeners moved to temporary garden plots in Magnuson Park, with the Children's Hospital agreeing to move 150 yards of soil from the former P-Patch to the new site (Magnuson Community Garden 2006d; Macdonald 2001).

DESIGN PROCESS AND IMPLEMENTATION: A GUIDING MASTER PLAN WITH INCREMENTALLY DESIGNED AREAS

The Magnuson Community Garden Coalition applied for and received support from the Small and Simple Projects Fund to develop a design in March 2000 (Magnuson Community Garden 2006c). Barker Landscape Architects, a local firm that had experience designing other Seattle community gardens, including Bradner Gardens Park, was hired through a Request for Proposals (RFP) process (Magnuson Community Garden 2006e). The design process was undertaken through steering committee meetings, three public meetings, and meetings with the Department of Parks and Recreation during the spring and summer of 2000 (Barker Landscape Architects 2000). The first public design meeting, in May 2000, centered on site understandings and creating design ideas; the second involved review of the design alternatives; and the third was a presentation of the final site plan(Magnuson Community Garden 2006f). A final concept design report was presented to the coalition in August 2000 (Magnuson Community Garden 2006e). The design was further refined through a second Small and Simple Projects Fund award. Both the Parks Department and the Seattle Design Commission reviewed the designs, and an environmental impact statement was prepared (Magnuson Community Garden 2006c).

The resulting plan addressed multiple uses through a "Bradner-type amalgam of activities," as well as interest in connecting to the park's community center and to local transitional housing (Macdonald 1999/2000; Magnuson Community Garden 2006b). Committees focused on various parts of the garden coordinated with Barker Landscape Architects to refine designs (DeMerritt 2002). For instance, a design charrette for the children's garden took place in October 2001, in which children participated. The Native Plant Committee advanced the design of the border, and the Magnuson Environmental Stewardship Alliance received a grant from the Department of Neighborhoods for 100 trees for the area. The garden's art committee held a design charrette in October 2002 for the P-Patch central open space. A tranquil garden committee worked with horticultural therapists on this garden's design (Magnuson Community Garden 2006d).

With a groundbreaking ceremony in February 2002, much of the garden's construction was underway. The construction company that moved the soil from the Sand Point P-Patch also contributed to the garden's development by demolishing existing asphalt and providing rough grading for the new garden (Magnuson Community Garden 2006d). By 2003, the path system, amphitheater terraces, and tranquil garden paving had been completed, as well as the P-Patch plots, native plant border, native plant nursery, and orchard (Magnuson Community Garden 2006g). In June 2004, a dedication was held for the arbor, with the amphitheater walls and grass in place (Magnuson Community Garden 2006h).

Even before the garden was fully constructed, there was cause to celebrate and promote the effort. An open house was held in February 2003, during which tours were given, participating groups displayed information, and volunteer opportunities were presented. Another open house was given that July as part of the city's thirtieth anniversary of the P-Patch Program (Magnuson Community Garden 2006g).

FUNDING AND SUPPORT: SEEKING FUNDING AND BROAD-BASED VOLUNTEER EFFORTS

To develop a community garden intended to serve such an array of public functions required effective fundraising as well as broad-based and continued volunteer involvement. It was the task of the Magnuson Community Garden Coalition to secure funding for the garden's design and development. The group received a $10,000 Small and Simple Projects Fund award to undertake the master plan. A second such award was received for construction drawings of the garden's utilities, landform, and drainage, and a $750 Neighborhood Outreach grant for a sign at the garden (Magnuson Community Garden 2006c, 2006i). The Garden received $118,000 from the Pro Parks Levy, as well as a Department of Neighborhoods Large Project Fund award of $150,000 that was matched with $244,814 in donations for a total cost estimated at $735,000 (Magnuson Community Garden 2006d).

With community match contributions, the garden has benefited from volunteer efforts and the contributions of numerous individuals and organizations. Numerous groups volunteered time—including EarthCorps, the Magnuson Environmental Stewardship Alliance, Youth for Peace, schoolchildren, and the Children's Hospital—and businesses and individuals contributed professional services and materials. Additionally, the garden received support from foundations and organizations, including the University Lions Club, the MJF Foundation, and the Captain Planet Foundation (Magnuson Community Garden 2006j). A grant from the Master Gardener Foundation was also awarded to the children's garden to build a toolshed, and the entrance structure to the children's garden was built by a local Eagle Scout Troop (Magnuson Community Garden 2006g, 2006k).

ORGANIZATION AND PARTICIPATION: MANAGING MULTIPLE GARDENS AS ONE

As an organization, the Magnuson Community Garden was granted nonprofit status in 2002 (Magnuson Community Garden 2006d). This organization is structured with a board of directors that works in cooperation with the Department of Parks and Recreation, which maintains oversight of the community garden's development. The board includes two ex officio members from the city: the director of Magnuson Park and the head of the P-Patch program. The Parks Department manages rental of the garden amphitheater, while garden volunteers manage the varied garden spaces. Committees address the park design, art, and each of the garden

9.7
A performance at the amphitheater brings many visitors to the garden. Photograph by Vanessa Lee, 2006.

9.8
Giving gardens, or food bank gardens, are located throughout the P-Patch. Photograph by Arielle Farina Clark, 2005.

spaces, and garden space committees organize work parties that are coordinated with the Parks Department (Magnuson Community Garden 2006l).

Volunteers can be involved through a myriad of regularly scheduled work parties, volunteer activities, and classes. The P-Patch holds monthly work parties from April through October. In addition, the children's garden has work parties one Saturday each month in the summer, as well as a harvest party in early fall. The native plant borders are maintained through work parties held every other Saturday. The native plant nursery has a work party once a month, offering volunteers insights on native plants as they assist with the plants. Summer composting workshops will assist with the garden's compost bins, and soil and vermiculture classes for families have been scheduled—both sponsored by Seattle Public Utilities' Master Composter/Soil Builder program (Magnuson Community Garden 2006m).

Within the P-Patch, a site coordinator provides overall leadership for garden work parties, the food bank beds, and communication between participants. The plots are organized into five groups, or what a gardener describes as "pods," each with varying numbers of plots, a compost bin, and food bank or "giving garden" plot. To ease communication, efforts are underway for each pod to have a leader to help coordinate garden maintenance. Lettuce Link, a program of the nonprofit Solid Ground addressing food security and urban agriculture, provides support for P-Patch food bank gardens.

PROGRAMS AND FUNCTIONS: SYNERGIES OF ACTIVITY

I've been there for a couple of concerts where it's just fun to be working in the garden. You know, working in the garden with jazz in the background is pretty exotic.
—A GARDENER

The varied garden features and functions effectively define the community garden as a multifaceted focal point in the midst of a metropolitan park that attracts gardeners and visitors alike. Some garden uses, such as the amphitheater, bring people who may not otherwise know of the garden, and those making use of adjacent park activities may be enticed by the garden's unique qualities.

Amphitheater

The concept of an amphitheater between the Community Activity Center building and gardens arose at initial design meetings. As realized, the amphitheater serves as the garden's formal hub, from which the other garden spaces may be reached. A path extends directly to the Community Activity Center, with a small triangle garden formed where this path and another one from the building meet a path that extends from the garden's south entry. A large circular green serves as a stage, with lawn terraces providing a semicircle of seating that is crowned by an arbor. The terraces are bisected by a stairway to the P-Patch Garden. The amphitheater is well-utilized in the summer, with concerts, theatrical performances, and educational programs, as well as weddings and other reserved events (Magnuson Community Garden 2006h).

P-Patch Garden

The P-Patch garden extends behind the amphitheater and to the north, with a centrally located gathering area. The gathering area contains informal seating and a sun dial. Paths lined with floral plantings meander through the garden. Paths connect through the native plant border to the perimeter road and continue west to the toolshed and compost area.

While not as culturally diverse as the other P-Patches, the Magnuson P-Patch has gardeners of many ages. One gardener is ninety-five and is the regular driver that takes produce to the local food bank. One family with young children has a sandbox to entertain the children. Gardeners interviewed drive or ride bicycles to the garden, which has ample parking nearby.

The gardeners interviewed conveyed a sense of community underway within the P-Patch, cultivated through casual conversations and shared activities. In addition to the communal labor of building the garden, current P-Patch gardeners share insights, seeds, and harvests. Work parties bring people together to improve and maintain common areas and features. Gardeners also tend plots dedicated to providing fresh food for a local food bank and for residents of the park's transitional housing program. Work efforts have been interspersed with celebrations, including summer solstice and fall equinox celebrations by some gardeners, and a garden-wide potluck that was enlivened by a marimba band performance at the amphitheater.

Children's Garden

On the southwestern side of the site lies the children's garden, with its entry marked by a post-and-beam threshold. The children's garden contains a small gathering area that is flanked by a playfully designed storage shed on one side and a mound garden with plants of varied textures and colors and paths lined with stones painted by children on the other. At the top of the mound is a circular space with log rounds for seating and mosaic-laid circular pavers. There is also a "rolling lawn" on one slope. A 2003 design activity generated a nautical motif, and gardens suggesting a whale and a starfish were created. The garden has a curriculum and teaching kits for teachers wishing to bring their classes there (Magnuson Children's Garden n.d.). During the monthly work parties from April to October, activities are provided for children in order to attract families (Magnuson Community Garden 2006m).

Native Plant Borders and the Native Plant Nursery

Native plants frame the community garden, and are grown for planting elsewhere. The native plant borders create a densely vegetated swath along the garden's eastern and southern edges and are punctuated with small garden entries and signs that describe native plants and their attributes. The native plant nursery at the northwest corner of the garden is managed by several groups. The plants are used in Magnuson Park restoration projects and elsewhere (Magnuson Community Garden 2006n).

9.9
The children's garden is enlivened by features such as this mosaic whale's tail, with the lush planted mound and shed behind providing other play and learning opportunities. Photograph by Leslie Gia Clark, 2007.

9.10
The tranquil garden is nestled into the slope in the background, with shrubs shaping a green enclave. Photograph by Leslie Gia Clark, 2007.

Tranquil Garden

Nestled into the garden's western slope, just north of the amphitheatre, lies a quiet paved courtyard. A low perimeter wall defines the space, with portions topped by a trellis-like fence and dense plantings in front. Movable tables and chairs provide opportunities for respite, and a stone fountain provides a focus in the garden.

Orchard

As one of the elements of the master plan, the orchard contains a mix of apple, pear, and plum trees as a demonstration garden for urban settings. In addition to the rows of trees, espaliers in three different patterns have been created near the children's garden (Magnuson Community Garden 2006o).

Other Features

In addition to these specific program elements, the entire garden features elements that create habitats for birds and other animals and welcome visitors. Alongside the main path, small ponds collect rainwater and also attract ducks and frogs. The sight and sound of birds animate the garden, and drilled boards have been posted throughout the garden to serve bees. The children's garden has served as a host to nests of killdeer, and hummingbirds, goldfinches, a frog, and butterflies have been spotted there as well (Magnuson Community Garden 2006k).

Building on the many aspects of the garden that enliven it, the Magnuson Community Garden group has drafted opportunities for further development in phase 3, following the design and construction phases. Areas such as the central open space within the P-Patch and the garden entrance have been targeted and ideas for the other garden spaces have been identified, including educational signs and links to other groups (Magnuson Community Garden 2006p).

CONTEXTUAL FACTORS AND CHALLENGES: NEIGHBORING ACTIVITY

While gardeners have described some instances of vandalism and theft, the garden seems to benefit from the activity of adjacent uses, such as the dog off-leash area. As one P-Patch gardener noted in choosing a location visible to the off-leash area, "There is no time day or night that there isn't somebody, that there aren't several cars there and things going on with the dogs." While a garden and dog off-leash area may seem incompatible, the gardener pointed out that the intervening native plant border has become established enough to discourage dogs from running into the garden.

SPECIAL LESSON: A COMMUNITY GARDEN ENRICHING A LARGE URBAN PARK

Given its location within a metropolitan park, the Magnuson Community Garden attracts other park users. One user commented, "We have many, many, many more visitors in any one day than we have gardeners." Another P-Patch gardener observed that "the public borders make it a really inviting place to walk. . . . It's amazing how many people walk. . . . All just out, and they want to chat about P-Patches."

While some gardeners seem to enjoy the popularity and openness of the garden, the solitude that was more readily available at the old Sand Point P-Patch was missed by one gardener in a *P-Patch Post* newsletter article: "When all of the 'community garden' is finally completed there will undoubtedly be various sorts of performances in the amphitheater, which will attract crowds of people who may then wander through the vegetable patches. Already we hear songs and chants of the summer day camps held just down the slope. One evening we heard the calls of a bingo game somewhere on the park grounds. And with the dogs and people in the nearby off-leash area, it is not a quiet place" (Bergelin 2003).

This article was preceded by an editor's note about a previous article that addressed issues of public-ness in community gardens, with an invitation for further dialogue. Indeed, the subsequent *P-Patch Post* featured a response from a gardener about the very public and mixed-use Bradner Gardens Park, celebrating

9.11
The park setting of the Magnuson Community Garden attracts other users to the garden. Photograph by Jeffrey Hou, 2005.

its diversity, and one from a Picardo P-Patch gardener, who described the quiet of this original P-Patch and offered an invitation to the Magnuson gardener (see Moty 2003; Alexander 2003).

While one of many features in Magnuson Park, the Magnuson Community Garden attracts people for multiple reasons. The amphitheater's events, including musical and dramatic performances as well as educational programs, draw many visitors and thus increase the visibility and public nature of the garden. These activities and nearby uses create a synergy with the garden. For example, children engaged in activities at the community center may come to the garden as one of their activities. As one gardener described the environment of the garden's context, "You want there to be a critical mass of the activity going on, and compared to the other P-Patches in town, this one is surrounded with it, in a different way."

Magnuson Community Garden provides valuable insights for multifunctional gardens to be realized within a park context. The coincidence of a large urban park being developed at a time when a nearby P-Patch was seeking a new home may be unique, yet this case demonstrates that community gardens can be successfully integrated and play a vital role within a park as habitat, a place of learning, a local source of nutrition and beauty, and a medium for community interaction.

PART III

LESSONS FROM SEATTLE

As urban open space with multiple and sometimes overlapping benefits and challenges, community gardens are complex places, from initial planning and design to implementation and ongoing maintenance. The development of community gardens typically depends on multiple actors and resources, which in turn generate a complex web of benefits beyond the scope of gardening. The dynamics of individuals and organizations, local politics, and the local economy are also factors that shape the ability of gardens to be sustained and evolve. In Seattle, as in many other cities, community gardens are appreciated resources. Yet even with the support of local government, the realities of scarce financial resources and marginalization as an urban land use require creative efforts to garner tangible support such as land security, funding, and program assistance. This creativity has been reflected in design solutions as well as in grassroots organizing and partnerships in Seattle. The Seattle experience highlights a range of persistent goals and challenges faced by urban community gardens. With challenges come opportunities to rethink support in terms of organizing, advocacy, and, more specifically, the capacities of planning and design.

As documented in part 2, the six case-study gardens in Seattle offer lessons and insights for making community gardens socially, economically, and environmentally sustainable places that support the health, nutrition, learning, and well-being of their users and the larger community. While significant variations exist across the different cases in terms of specific contexts, constraints, and available resources, several consistent themes emerge. Chapter 10 provides a comparison of the approaches of different gardens that respond to the needs of different communities and locations. Through the physical design of the gardens and the processes of development and maintenance, these gardens provide a range of social, environmental, educational, and economic benefits that echo the multiple dimensions of urban sustainability. By using sustainability as the framework for analysis, the urban community garden can be understood as serving a range of desirable social and environmental outcomes at the city scale. However, while successful community gardens exist, there are also persistent challenges, including larger political and economic forces, as well as issues particular to each garden. It is therefore the focus of this chapter to highlight both the opportunities and the challenges facing urban community gardens from the perspective of sustainability.

As places that experience seasonal changes and evolve with the people who garden the plots, community gardens require special care in design and planning. Chapter 11 focuses on the community garden as a hybrid public space that facilitates multiple uses and functions. The chapter highlights selected lessons in planning and design while also raising some considerations for a larger support structure drawn from professionals, city agencies, nonprofit organizations, and others. Chapter 12 concludes with a vision of urban community gardens as an organizing concept that serves individuals, neighborhoods, and city regions. It further outlines steps necessary for this vision to be realized.

10

Expressions and Challenges of Sustainability

As noted in part 1, community gardens have often been portrayed as expressions of urban sustainability because of the many personal, social, economic, and environmental benefits they potentially provide. While this supposition may be intuitively trusted by those who are involved in community gardening, our goal in this book is to critically analyze how community gardens achieve dimensions of urban sustainability. Specifically, in the Seattle cases, how are the broad concepts of sustainability actually translated into tangible actions and physical expressions in the gardens? What are the ingredients behind the successful aspects of cases in Seattle? What are the challenges to sustaining community gardens as well as making them an embodiment of urban sustainability?

MULTIPLE EXPRESSIONS OF URBAN SUSTAINABILITY

The selected cases from Seattle provide some grounded insights into and evidences of the multiple connections between urban community gardens and the concept and practice of sustainability. Specifically, they show how the development, maintenance, and programming of the gardens are closely associated with the social, economic, and environmental dimensions of urban sustainability. Through the provision of space for gardening, their public nature, and complementary program development to extend learning opportunities, community gardens provide resources and opportunities to promote sustainable practices at the levels of neighborhood, district, and city. The following highlights how the case-study gardens in Seattle provide different expressions of urban sustainability and how their synthesis is equally critical to success.

People and Social Sustainability

Each P-patch is only as good as its coordinators.
—A GARDENER

One of the key ingredients behind the success of community gardens in Seattle is the people. The making and maintenance of a community garden, whether big or small, new or old, often involve a wide range of actors and stakeholders, including gardeners, site coordinators, agency staff, professionals, neighbors, and countless volunteers from both inside and outside the garden's community. For every community garden there is a story about how gardeners, staff, volunteers, and professionals have worked together to plan, design, and manage the gardens; how they have mobilized personal and collective networks; and how they have reached out to neighbors and outside organizations. There are shared stories of how the process of making the gardens in turn builds communities, and vice versa. Behind each garden, there are dedicated individuals that make things happen by coordinating volunteers, writing grant proposals, identifying problems and resources, settling disputes, and helping with everyday maintenance.

The social communities associated with the gardens often grow beyond the gardeners and the garden's immediate neighbors. At the Danny Woo Community Garden, for example, the garden was first built by a group of neighborhood activists with help from outside professionals, volunteers, and businesses. Today, the garden continues the tradition by involving generations of gardeners, university students, and volunteers throughout the city. Bradner Gardens Park is another example in which a coalition of individuals and organizations contributed to the initial creation of the park and continued to work together in managing both the park and the gardens. The process brought together longtime residents and refugees, who made the garden a sanctuary in their newly adopted home. Even in cases such as Interbay and Thistle, where many gardeners are not from the immediate neighborhoods, the garden provides a place for social gathering and community building that expands beyond geographical ties to a place.

Building and sustaining social ties is essential to the development and maintenance of community gardens. To sustain activism and involvement, many garden groups organize events and activities to engage gardeners and volunteers. Work parties are a common practice; they not only coordinate volunteer activities and realize development projects but also encourage gardeners and volunteers to work together and rely on each other. Some gardens are particularly known for their unique social events. For example, Interbay P-Patch has "Saturday soup socials"

Table 10.1.
List of social and community activities

INTERBAY P-PATCH	• annual salmon barbeque
	• seasonal gatherings: Christmas wreath-making, New Year's dinner, solstice party, Fourth of July party
	• special events (Jazz in the Garden, Big Fat Greek Picnic)
	• fundraisers (dahlia plant sale, honey sale)
	• tours, workshops, and teaching
	• compost/Saturday soup socials
	• Friday night potlucks
THISTLE P-PATCH	• volunteer workdays
DANNY WOO INTERNATIONAL DISTRICT COMMUNITY GARDEN	• tours and workshops
	• volunteer workdays (1-2 per month)
	• annual pig roast
BRADNER GARDENS PARK	• tours, workshops, and demonstrations
	• children's garden activities
	• plant sales
	• occasional concerts
	• annual events: New Year's Eve burn, Halloween party, Fourth of July party
MARRA FARM	• volunteer workdays
	• annual Fall Fest
MAGNUSON P-PATCH	• open-house events (first year)
	• children's garden activities
	• amphitheater events: music, drama, etc.
	• volunteer workdays

and an annual salmon barbeque; the Danny Woo Community Garden invites members of the broader community to celebrate the history of community activism at its annual pig roast; and Bradner Gardens Park has a July Fourth fireworks party, a Halloween party, and a New Year's burn. Through announcements in P-Patch newsletters and posted on information boards at the gardens, the wider community can also learn about these events and choose to participate. These activities expand

the opportunities for involvement to the community at large and make the gardens a gathering place for a broader urban population. In many ways, just as the community builds the garden, the garden builds the community and strengthens the social ties among gardeners, neighbors, activists, and citizens.

Food and Economic Sustainability

Because of this garden, we are able to grow mostly vegetables that we use in Japanese cooking. And that is a huge difference in both taste and how far our household economy goes.

—A GARDENER AT BRADNER

In Seattle, although community gardens can be found in both affluent and poor neighborhoods, they play a particularly important role as a food source for low-income families, recent refugees, and immigrants. In these communities, vegetables and fruits grown at the gardens supplement the families' diets and allow them to spend less of their disposable income on food. For refugees and immigrants with limited employable skills, gardening is an activity that allows them to be economically productive and provides stability in a time of transition. In gardens such as Thistle, Danny Woo, Marra Farm, and Bradner, food production not only meets

10.1
Events such as the Annual Fall Fest at Marra Farm are important in building community among gardeners. Photograph by Vanessa Lee, 2005.

10.2
The Annual Harvest Banquet gathers gardeners and P-Patch staff to enjoy a unique potluck meal together. Photograph by Vanessa Lee, 2005.

10.3
Produce from the Seattle Youth Garden Works' plots at Marra Farm contributes to the local food bank. Photograph by Vanessa Lee, 2006.

the nutritional and social needs of the gardeners but also contributes to economic sustainability in communities that the gardens serve.

Another aspect of community food security is the capacity of gardeners to share their produce with others. In many of the case-study gardens, there are volunteers who grow food for the local food bank. Lettuce Link, a local food and garden program serving low-income people, in particular has a presence in community gardens throughout the city. Gardeners and volunteers at Magnuson, Interbay, Marra, and many other community gardens contribute tons of fresh produce to area food banks. Not only is healthy food provided, but the experience is educational and social for the volunteers.

Additionally, special community garden programs provide low-income immigrants and at-risk youth with skills. In particular, Seattle Youth Garden Works manages a garden at Marra Farm that engages teams of local at-risk youth in science education while raising produce to sell at local farmers' markets and to contribute to a local food bank. Within Seattle Housing Authority properties, the Cultivating Communities program (described in chapter 3) includes Community Supported Agriculture gardening, wherein gardeners receive income through subscriptions for their collective produce.

Gardening and Cultural Sustainability

Well, my family are farmers. So we've been farming for a long time, for a few generations already. So I guess it's in the blood already.
—A GARDENER

Along with contributing to economic sustainability, community gardens also provide important opportunities for cultural sustainability. In immigrant communities in particular, gardeners provide opportunities for new immigrants to continue their cultural traditions of food production, diet, cooking, and socializing. The practice is most evident in gardens such as Danny Woo, Thistle, Marra Farm, and Bradner, where there are significant immigrant populations. In these gardens, one can easily distinguish unique vegetables and plants and unusual cultivation practices. The gardens on these sites provide a way for many of the gardeners to retain connections to their cultural traditions. Childhood memories of working with parents on a farm return as gardeners work in a new environment. In many of these gardens, garden-

10.4
Gardening allows for both the continuation of agricultural traditions and the raising of new crops (High Point). Photograph by Vanessa Lee, 2007.

ers grow vegetables that are hard to find or tend to be more expensive in stores and supermarkets. Some gardens that were first started by first-generation immigrants are now tended by their children, and traditions and knowledge are passed down from one generation to another.

Community gardens in the immigrant communities also provide a chance for immigrant families and individuals to sustain cultural communities. In the International District, the Danny Woo Community Garden provides one of few places in the community where elderly immigrants in particular can go and meet each other. The gardens provide opportunities for those arriving as individuals or couples to interact with others, make friends, and develop social networks. At Thistle, gardening also provides opportunities for individuals to get out of their apartments and houses and to socialize with others. This has been particularly important for immigrant and refugee families, who do not have other networks for meeting people and seeking help. As social settings, community gardens provide opportunities for immigrant gardeners to share information and tips that can help in their adjustment to a new environment. The gardens provide an important source of stability and continuity for immigrant families in a new environment.

Placemaking and Neighborhood Sustainability

As a way of utilizing vacant and residual lands, urban community gardens also play an important role in the physical improvement and revitalization of neighborhoods. Many of the community gardens in Seattle make effective use of unused or marginal lands and thus contribute to the positive transformation of the neighborhoods in which they are located. For example, Bradner Gardens Park was a reinvestment on underutilized park property. Interbay P-Patch was developed on a capped landfill in an industrial corridor. The Danny Woo Community Garden was built on a land-locked, steeply sloped vacant parcel that was difficult to develop. Thistle P-Patch made use of a utility corridor under power lines. Marra Farm transformed fallow agricultural land at the outskirts of the city into an active garden and neighborhood open space that supports both informal recreational and programmed gardening activities. These gardens provide rare green open spaces in a dense urban environment. They have also made underutilized lands in the respective neighborhoods into important social and environmental assets.

By transforming underutilized lands into active space, community gardens provide important gathering places that in turn strengthen social connections among neighbors and gardeners. For instance, Bradner Gardens Park is a multiuse space that attracts gardeners and neighbors alike. Social activities play an important role at the Interbay P-Patch. And the Danny Woo Community Garden is a social gathering place for the elderly residents in the neighborhood. Because many of the gardens have been created through community efforts, they provide tangible, posi-

10.5
The Danny Woo
Community Garden
turns a vacant hillside
into a community asset.
Photograph by Jeffrey
Hou, 2006.

Table 10.2.
Program elements for neighborhood and community

INTERBAY P-PATCH	• site open to public • garden courtyard ("plaza") • compost center • food bank gardens • public toilet • fountain with information kiosk • social events
THISTLE P-PATCH	• site open to public
DANNY WOO INTERNATIONAL DISTRICT COMMUNITY GARDEN	• site open to public • social spaces, benches, and viewing kiosks • pig-roasting pit • adjacent to Kobe Terrace Park
BRADNER GARDENS PARK	• site open to public • social spaces and benches • art pieces • pavilion • children's play area • basketball court • public toilet • open lawn • meeting room • information board and signs
MARRA FARM	• site open to public • daylighted creek • interpretive signage (some bilingual) • picnic tables • public toilet • information boards and signs
MAGNUSON P-PATCH	• site open to public • gardening within a metropolitan park • adjacent to park's Community Activity Center • children's garden • tranquil garden • native plant garden • native plant nursery • food bank gardens • gathering area and benches • amphitheater with free scheduled performances • informational signs

10.6
Artists and residents in Seattle's Belltown neighborhood converted a vacant lot into a community garden and preserved it as an open space that has since served a growing downtown residential neighborhood. Photograph by Jeffrey Hou, 2005.

tive examples of what the community can achieve if members and stakeholders work together to find creative solutions. Such engagement often enables diverse, multicultural, and multigenerational populations to interact and learn from one another. As such, community gardens improve both the quality of life and the social connections in urban neighborhoods.

Learning and Environmental Sustainability

As places to grow food, connect with nature, and create functional habitats, community gardens provide opportunities for learning that contribute to environmental sustainability in an urban setting. Gardens allow urban residents to experience environmental phenomena and processes that are often lost in a developed urban setting. In the gardens, awareness of seasonal, hydrological, and nutrient cycles may be gained through the informal day-to-day experiences of gardening, interpretive events, and formalized classes and workshops. In the Seattle cases, the practices of organic gardening, recycling, composting; the application and demonstration of sustainable technology such as rainwater harvesting and solar and wind energy; and educational workshops and activities also provide opportuni-

Table 10.3.
Environmental learning programs and elements

INTERBAY P-PATCH	• compost classes • food bank garden/workshops • food bank garden partnerships with high-school class and university students • tours for schools and other groups
THISTLE P-PATCH	• informal instructions by site coordinator
DANNY WOO INTERNATIONAL DISTRICT COMMUNITY GARDEN	• organic gardening workshop for elderly • tours for schools and other groups
BRADNER GARDENS PARK	• Master Gardener workshops • Seattle Tilth workshops • composting workshops • demonstration areas • green building: building materials, solar and water harvesting • interpretive signs
MARRA FARM	• interpretive signs (some bilingual) • garden shelter and cleaning/food-prep station • educational program with local school • educational program for at-risk youth
MAGNUSON P-PATCH	• children's garden • native plant garden with signage

ties for learning. As programs engage people of all ages, peer and intergenerational learning may be fostered.

Many of the gardens in Seattle have become examples of local best practices in environmental sustainability. Some gardens actively promote the use of organic fertilizers and water conservation by using compost and drought-tolerant plants. In gardens with a large presence of immigrant gardeners, additional efforts have been made to share information through translation and interpretation. Many programs also reach out to the larger general public with educational workshops and activities,. In Seattle, local government agencies and nonprofit organizations are aware of the potential of outreach and education at the community gardens and have been strong supporters of various programs to promote sustainable practices in gardening, composting, and energy and resource conservation. For example,

10.7
(above, left)
Facilities such as this
one at Bradner Gardens
Park help promote the
practice of composting.
Photograph by Vanessa
Lee, 2005.

10.8
(above, right)
Rainwater barrels at the Cascade P-Patch
promote sustainable practices in urban
community gardens. Photograph by Jeffrey
Hou, 2005.

10.9
"If the wheel is turning to the left
(backwards), the solar panels are generating
electricity to the 'grid.'" As a solar energy
demonstration, Bradner Gardens Park
generates not only food but energy.
Photograph by Vanessa Lee, 2005.

Bradner Gardens Park includes demonstration solar panels that were provided by
the local utility company. The environmental learning programs and facilities at
Bradner—including workshops and classes, organic gardening, children's garden,
demonstration gardens, and green building technologies—also receive support
from public and nonprofit organizations.

Health and Individual Well-Being

Besides the collective social, economic, and environmental benefits of community
gardens, the case studies in Seattle also demonstrate the importance of gardening
for the physical and psychological well-being of individuals. In our interviews, com-

10.10
Gardening in the Danny Woo Community Garden provides an important opportunity for the elderly population in an urban setting to engage in physical activities. Photograph by Vanessa Lee, 2006.

munity gardeners and site coordinators consistently highlighted the therapeutic aspect of gardening—especially the delight and satisfaction of seeing plants grow and flourish. For many gardeners, the gardens provide a physical and psychological refuge in dense and busy urban settings. For immigrants and refugees in particular, the gardens provide both economic and psychological relief from the stress of everyday life in a new environment.

In addition to their therapeutic benefits, community gardens enable a more active lifestyle. As a walkable destination for recreation or gardening, gardens such as Bradner that are located within a residential neighborhood also inspire local residents to walk and engage in more physical activities. Other gardens may be less accessible to users on foot, but gardeners may come on bicycle, as do some at the Magnuson Community Garden. This garden's predecessor, Sand Point P-Patch, was adjacent to the metropolitan Burke-Gilman Trail, which is heavily used by bicyclists and pedestrians, and was thus more accessible. For elderly gardeners who often have no other opportunities to engage in physical activities or to leave their apartments and homes, community gardens provide important opportunities for more active living. At the Danny Woo Community Garden, the elderly gardeners express the desire to check on the gardens every day. They also appreciate the health benefit of even just walking to the garden. At Thistle, elderly immigrant gardeners are there on an almost full-time basis. At both sites, one can find gardeners who are over seventy years of age and who continue to be active in the gardens.

10.11
Student volunteers are an important source of support for community gardens such as Marra Farm. Photograph by Vanessa Lee, 2005.

Diversity, Interconnections, and Program Sustainability

As described above, the community gardens in Seattle embody the multidimensionality of sustainability in an urban environment. As in an ecosystem, the diverse aspects and processes in a community garden are interconnected and interdependent. For example, the economic benefits of the gardens are linked with the cultural and environmental benefits through organic food production. The social and environmental aspects of gardening are linked through organized maintenance and educational activities. The individual benefits of the gardens would not be possible without collective efforts in creating, maintaining, and improving the gardens. The success of each garden reflects collaborative efforts by the community at large. Because the benefits are interconnected and interdependent, the contributions of the community gardens to different dimensions of urban sustainability are also linked with the sustainability of the gardens themselves.

In different circumstances and through different approaches, each of the case-study gardens has brought together individuals and organizations that are responsible for different aspects of the gardens. These individuals and organizations bring diverse sets of skills and resources—including funding, technical expertise, volunteer labor, and additional institutional and social networks—to mobilize other resources. At all of the gardens, partnerships have been created between local government agencies, nonprofit organizations, community groups, design and planning professionals, and local schools or university students and faculty. They ensure not only the continuing operation of the gardens but also the educational, social, and nutritional programs that expand the benefits of the gardens.

At Bradner Gardens Park, a coalition of neighborhood activists and nonprofit organizations was critical to preserving the park land and leading the design and planning of the park to include multiple programs. Similarly, the design and planning of gardens at Magnuson Park and Marra Farm also were led by coalitions of groups. Places such as Thistle P-Patch and Danny Woo Community Gardens, while relying more on individuals and neighborhood organizations, also drew on multiple resources and networks for funding, expertise, and volunteers. These individuals and organizations bring more than just financial support; they also bring the social, institutional, and political capital to sustain the gardens and ensure that they continue to fulfill multiple roles in the neighborhoods and communities at large.

CHALLENGES FOR URBAN COMMUNITY GARDENS

Last year, someone came into my shed, and the shed was locked good, and somebody just hit the lock and broke the lock and came inside and searched through everything. I don't have anything valuable. Only tools.
—A GARDENER AT THISTLE

Despite demonstrated benefits and strong institutional support, community gardens in Seattle continue to face a series of persistent challenges that range from external constraints, such as impermanent uses and vandalism, to internal challenges that result from organizational uncertainty and intercultural differences. These persistent challenges highlight specific issues associated with contemporary American cities, the continuing struggle of the community garden movement, and the need for particular support in order to sustain the functions and benefits of urban community gardens for the gardeners and the broader urban communities.

Impermanent Use

In spite of support from the city administration and from many community and nonprofit organizations, most community gardens in Seattle still do not have permanent use of the space they occupy. The impermanent nature of community gardens has been a perennial problem that often results in the relocation of gardens and occasional threats of displacement. The Interbay P-Patch in particular was moved twice to accommodate development of a public golf course on city-owned land. It was saved only because of the persistence and perseverance of the gardeners. The Sand Point P-Patch also was moved to its current Magnuson Park location after the property owner, the Children's Hospital, terminated the lease for the garden in order to use the site for a new building. The Thistle P-Patch occupies a utility right-of-way under a temporary-use permit. The Danny Woo Community Garden was created by a verbal agreement with a private landowner and currently occupies a city property through an agreement with city agencies. At Marra Farm, the site is being used and managed by a coalition of groups that do not own the property. Bradner Gardens Park would not have come to existence, and its preceding community garden would have been lost, if community activists and garden advocates had not organized a grassroots campaign and fought the city's plan to sell the site for real estate development.

In light of growing popularity and recognition of the benefits of community gardens in a park setting, the Seattle Department of Parks and Recreation has established a policy permitting P-Patches as a recreational use in parks. Additionally, a Memorandum of Agreement (MOA) with the Department of Parks and Recreation has been developed for some gardens, including those where multiple groups are involved, such as Bradner Gardens Park. Although the policy and MOA facilitate conditional use of park land for community gardens, an arrangement of this kind still falls short of permanent protection for the gardens. The impermanent status often subjects the gardens to potential changes, particularly in the face of development and/or scrutiny by neighbors and other local authorities. Sometimes the conditions imposed on the community gardens by temporary-use permits have prevented the building of permanent structures that could provide much-needed service space for the maintenance and operation of the gardens. As a result of these limitations, which often give the gardens a makeshift appearance, community gardens continue to be treated as a temporary use of land.

The movement toward self-ownership with land-trust arrangements under the P-Patch Trust indicates a desire for more permanent and stable community gardens in Seattle. In addition to the need to purchase sites, there is a fundamental need for more coordinated planning and policy making at the citywide level to ensure that community gardens become a legitimate land use category, similar to parks and other types of open space. In cases involving the use of infrastructure corridors, rights-of-way, and existing open space for community gardens, co-management mechanisms can also be established or further refined to ensure stability and mutual benefits.

Resource Uncertainty

Despite institutional support from the city, as well as networks of resources in terms of expertise, funding, and volunteers, community gardeners in Seattle are challenged to acquire sufficient and stable resources for the gardens' continued maintenance and improvement. Many gardens rely heavily and sometimes exclusively on volunteer support. The coordination of volunteer efforts often imposes a heavy burden on a few core individuals who are volunteers themselves. Sustaining the energy and motivation necessary for the operation and maintenance of the gardens is a daily and challenging task. Gardens such as Thistle P-Patch and Danny Woo Community Gardens are fortunate to have paid staff support through neighborhood organizations and partnership with local agencies. But even in these cases, the individuals in charge are only able to maintain the day-to-day operation of the gardens. Any additional improvements require seeking outside grants and support,

10.12
Gardens are often the result of hard work by volunteers and multiple sources of funding (Bradner Gardens Park). Photograph by Jeffrey Hou, 2005.

which places additional burdens upon those individuals and creates uncertainty about the development and maintenance of the gardens.

This lack of stable funding, coupled with heavy reliance on volunteer efforts, creates discrepancy among community gardens in the city. Gardens with more active members and volunteers and more skillful coordinators are able to obtain more resources for maintenance and improvements. On the other hand, gardens with less active organizing are disadvantaged in receiving support. For example, while gardens such as Bradner Gardens Park can call upon the skills of lawyers, artists, horticulturists, and designers, not all garden groups are able to mobilize the same level of support and resources. While grants that require community involvement offer incentives for gardeners to mobilize and become more actively involved, the requirement may create a barrier for garden groups that do not have strong social capital to begin with. Limited funding also creates competition among gardens. Together with impermanent use of land, the lack of stable support puts many gardens at a loss for both short-term improvements and long-term planning.

Crime and Vandalism

Like most urban open spaces, community gardens in the Seattle cases are also vulnerable to crimes and vandalism. In Seattle, these problems are particularly acute for the P-Patch gardens because they are required to be publicly accessible. While public access contributes to the use of gardens as public open space, it is difficult to prevent the problems often associated with urban settings. For example, it has been a daily struggle to prevent drug dealing and drug use in Kobe Terrace Park from spilling over into the adjacent Danny Woo Community Garden. Theft of vegetables also causes frustration and anger among the gardeners. In gardens such as Interbay P-Patch, Thistle P-Patch and the Danny Woo Community Garden, theft has been a particular problem, reflecting the challenges of specific neighborhood contexts. At the Danny Woo Community Garden, theft has almost been accepted as part of everyday life. At Thistle, problems with theft have caused tensions and misunderstanding among gardeners. At the Interbay P-Patch, the presence of homeless people who were thought to be stealing from the garden led to several strategies, including encouraging the homeless to become plot gardeners themselves. However, the group's attitude could shift to more defensive approaches due to more recent problems with theft and vandalism.

10.13
A sign at the Bradner Gardens Park is used to deter theft. Photograph by Vanessa Lee, 2005.

The proximity of gardens to communities and neighborhoods can provide mutual benefits, but it can also be a source of conflict. While community gardens are meant to serve communities, not all community gardens involve the local residents. Sometimes differences between local residents and gardeners can result in different expectations and can create barriers to communication. At Thistle P-Patch and Marra Farm, tensions between gardeners and the immediate neighbors reflect the complexity in programming urban open space. At Thistle, the intensity of food production precludes the use of the land for social space or community gathering. Neighbors are annoyed by the makeshift appearance and the marginal location that they feel makes the site prone to dumping. At Marra Farm, conflicts between dog walkers and gardeners need to be negotiated as part of a larger neighborhood need for recreational activities. In many cases, mediating conflicts and outreach become a particular challenge when cultural barriers are present. As urban neighborhoods and gardens become more culturally diverse, differences in language and cultural customs present additional challenges.

Internal and Intercultural Conflicts

Like any social organization, community gardens also face interpersonal and organizational challenges. These include tensions that arise from different styles of gardening by individuals, occasional conflicts between neighboring gardeners, and sometimes intercultural conflicts among gardeners and between gardeners and garden managers. In some gardens, language barriers and cultural differences have caused misunderstandings among individuals and groups. Traditional ways of gardening for one group may not be discernable to others. Plots that involve a less formal way of gardening may be perceived as being messy and disorganized to gardeners from a different culture. These interpersonal and cultural differences and conflicts affect the social dynamics in the garden and put extra burdens on site coordinators to negotiate and resolve the conflicts.

While multiple uses of the garden bring mutual benefits to the garden and the community, they can also be sources of internal conflict. For example, at Magnuson P-Patch, one gardener has publicly complained about the lack of privacy in gardening in such a public context. At Bradner Gardens Park, there was some initial disagreement over the inclusion of a basketball court in the park. At the Danny Woo Community Garden, the gardeners and garden manager are constantly struggling with maintaining public access into the garden while deterring crime and drug activities.

Although these issues present a challenge to the gardens, they also create opportunities for dialogue with regard to the functions and nature of community gardens. The concerns of the Magnuson gardener expressed in an article in the *P-Patch Post* newsletter motivated other gardeners to write about the varied qualities of their gardens and to reflect on the issue. In debating the benefits of having a basketball court at Bradner, the gardeners and site coordinators came to realize the multiple perspectives and needs of different users in the park. In the end, the discussion led to better mutual understanding and shared goals for the garden. There are not quick solutions to many of the internal challenges to community gardens. However, the Seattle cases show that the challenges can also provide opportunities for discussion, collective action, and creative solutions.

11

Designing and Supporting Urban Community Gardens as Hybrid Public Space

I think when you're initially setting up an area, community garden, or berm or community spaces, an architect might play an important role in giving you guidance and direction. But once the garden is kind of set in concrete in many ways, then it's up to the community.
—A GARDENER AT INTERBAY P-PATCH

Much like the complex web of benefits and challenges, the design and programming of the case-study gardens in Seattle also offer a rich variety of lessons, as each garden faces a specific set of issues, including site-specific concerns and the need for creative solutions in light of scarce resources. The cases here demonstrate a range of opportunities and approaches that respond to different social issues and physical contexts. Some solutions have been perfected over the years and are being replicated, while others are still being tested and may need future revision. This chapter highlights some selected lessons in planning and design that stand out in the Seattle community garden case studies. It also raises some considerations for a larger support structure drawn from professionals, city agencies, nonprofit organizations, and others. This network of support is essential to the development, maintenance, and sustainability of community gardens. The concept of "hybrid public space" is introduced here to encapsulate the multifaceted conditions and considerations in the design and programming of urban community gardens.

DESIGN LESSONS: REFLECTING CONTEXT AND USER NEEDS

Danny Woo is completely funky, ethnic, and ad hoc, and [Bradner] is so groomed
and perfect.
—A DESIGNER

The first lesson that the Seattle case studies offer is that there are many models
of urban community gardens and each may require a different design response.
Some gardens are predominantly used for leisure and recreation, while others are
primarily used for food production. While one garden may be exclusively used for
gardening, another may combine gardening with other activities and uses. There
are gardens located in residential neighborhoods, in industrial areas, in transitional
zones between districts, and in marginal and underutilized land, as well as in prime
downtown locations. Some gardens are easily accessible while others are not. Some
require only simple construction and have minimal design features, while others are
more fully equipped with facilities and amenities.

The different models of urban community gardens involve different processes
for programming and design. Some require extensive participatory processes that
involve gardeners and neighbors in workshops and charrettes. Others are the result
of ad hoc efforts and informal involvement. Almost all gardens have gone through
incremental changes as a result of funding cycles, as well as adjustments and
improvements over time. The variety of responses reflects the specific conditions of
the site, the neighborhood, the needs of the gardeners, and the available resources.
They also reflect how involved a specific group of stakeholders is in the design and
programming process. As seen in the selected case studies in Seattle, an effective
process involves understanding the multiple variables and engaging the stakeholders
so that they can articulate their needs and participate in the actual implementation.

At Bradner Gardens Park, for example, the involvement of multiple stakeholder
groups led to a master plan that embraces both park and garden elements in the
same place. At the Danny Woo Community Garden, students in the design/build
studio first listened to gardeners' needs and desires and then developed schemes
that reflected the cultures of the specific ethnic populations that the garden served.
At Thistle P-Patch, a simple design satisfied the gardeners' needs for clear plot
boundaries and the maximization of gardening area to support intensive food production. By responding to the particular needs of the users, these approaches to
design and programming also reaffirm the unique identity of each garden. Comparisons between the Thistle P-Patch and Bradner Gardens Park in particular highlight
the different populations served, site contexts, programmatic intentions, and
resources. It is clear that Bradner is more elaborately designed to serve as a multiuse
park. However, the design at Thistle is equally appropriate to the specific needs of
its gardeners in terms of food production and related economic supplements.

11.1
Bradner Gardens Park
serves a broad community
by blending together
community gardens
and recreational uses.
Photograph by Jeffrey
Hou, 2005.

11.2
The Thistle P-Patch is
predominantly used for
food production and
reflects the primary
needs of its immigrant
and refugee gardeners.
Photograph by Arielle
Farina Clark, 2005.

Mediating Multiple Uses and Outreach

Multiple uses in community gardens are often the result of having multiple constituents and stakeholders. With the exception of Thistle P-Patch, all of the gardens in the selected case studies involve some combination of multiple uses. Multiuse becomes a necessary feature especially when gardens are located inside larger parks or open spaces that invite nongardening activities, as in the case of Magnuson Community Garden and Bradner Gardens Park. At Bradner Gardens Park, for example, the P-Patch plots share space with a lawn area, a playground, and a basketball court that serve different users and populations. In other cases, additional uses and activities directly relate to gardening. At Interbay P-Patch, for example, gardeners receive additional resources through the inclusion of beehives, toolsheds, composting areas, social spaces, and food bank facilities.

In cases where there are multiple uses, successful design and programming plays an important role in mediating potential conflicts among the different uses. At Bradner Gardens Park, sculptural fences and mosaic benches creatively and successfully resolved a potential conflict between the garden plots and recreational areas. Initially resisted by some, it later became apparent that the basketball court and playground provided benefits to the garden and gardeners. Specifically, they allowed gardeners to bring their children to the garden while also increasing the use of the park by nongardeners. Other areas inside Bradner Gardens Park, such as the central pavilion, the perimeter walk, and the open lawn, provide opportunities for nongardeners to use the park. At the Danny Woo Community Garden, while the garden serves mainly elderly gardeners, various seating structures and viewing platforms also provide places for nongardeners to use the garden and make an inviting open space for the neighborhood. Sensitive and creative design responses in these cases allow multiple uses to coexist and sometimes complement each other.

When outreach to the surrounding neighborhood is a challenge, incorporating other uses may motivate nongardeners to participate. For instance, to address the current conflict between Thistle gardeners and the adjacent community, it may be desirable to create places that can also be used by the adjacent community without displacing valuable gardening space. Similarly, additional demand for recreational space at Marra Farm has required clarification in programming and site planning, which has been underway. Mediating potential conflicts and producing synergetic effects are both challenges and opportunities in the programming and design of garden sites. As is evident at Bradner Gardens Park, a balance of gardening and nongardening uses can be achieved with creative programming and design solutions.

Multicultural Expressions through Design

The Southeast Asian gardeners have a whole different style. The way that they garden...seems very unstructured and chaotic to my eyes. But the more you look at it, the more you realize that there's a plan.
—A SITE COORDINATOR

A garden reflects the cultures of its gardeners. In the Seattle case studies, different garden designs signify the demographic and cultural backgrounds of their gardeners. In gardens such as Danny Woo, there is an explicit attempt in the design of common structures to reflect the cultural traditions and identities of the predominantly East Asian gardeners. At Thistle, individual huts built by gardeners not only serve functional needs but also create a strong cultural

11.3
Creative fence design at Bradner Gardens Park separates the basketball court from the garden and at the same time provides visual access and expression of the urban farm aesthetic. Photograph by Jeffrey Hou, 2006.

identity and character for the garden. In both cases, the structures play an important role in creating a sense of place in the garden and allow the gardeners to feel at home.

Although design can play an important role in helping to express the cultural identities of the gardens and the gardeners, it is important to be aware that culture expression involves more than overt cultural iconography on physical structures. In the Seattle case studies, the act of gardening itself—through different methods of cultivating, spatial arrangement, and choice of crops—is also an important cultural expression. In gardens with multicultural gardeners, such as Marra Farm and Bradner Gardens Park, one may find different cultivating methods and choices of vegetables and crops, reflecting different cultural traditions and ethnic backgrounds. The cultivating methods are sometimes reflected in the organization of the plots. Some appear to have more structure; others less so, to the undiscerning eye.

Understanding the different modes of gardening as cultural expressions and practices is important in design considerations as well as in mediating potential conflicts. Sometimes these practices do not require specific design requirements but rather the flexibility to allow individual modifications and adaptations. At other times, iconography may be desirable as an expression of identity and pride, and may encourage familiarity. To decide on specific strategies, designers and organizers should work with the gardeners to find out what these cultural practices are and how to best support them through design.

As user-initiated places, community gardens do not privilege professionals over nonprofessionals. Rather, they allow different knowledge and traditions to thrive and to influence the evolution of the space. As a result, the gardens are often reflective of the cultural preferences of the users. They provide places where the multiculturalism of contemporary cities can be supported and expressed. They

11.5
Gardeners' huts at the Thistle P-Patch provide shelter and storage for individual gardeners and function also as a cultural expression. Photograph by Arielle Farina Clark, 2005.

bring together "strangers in the city" and "multiple publics" to interact with each other and find individual and collective refuges in an urban environment.

Too Much or Too Little Design?

The garden is *never done*. It's a work in progress.
—A GARDEN MANAGER

While a significant number of community gardens in the Seattle case studies involve deliberate design efforts, most gardens evolve by incremental adjustments. This incremental nature of garden development, often resulting from scarce resources and the involvement of volunteer labor, produces a unique organic quality. Such developments can present a dilemma for design. On one hand, when gardens are excessively designed, individual creativity may be stifled and later adaptations that facilitate use and sense of ownership may be hindered. Excessive design also prevents the gardeners and community from investing their own efforts in the garden. It impedes the community-building process. On the other hand, lack of investment in design and building of permanent structures can further marginalize the status of community gardens as a legitimate type of land use.

In Seattle, obstacles to garden design and improvements include limited resources and institutional barriers against building permanent structures on temporary sites. The absence of design often contributes to a lack of identity and amenities for some gardens and makes it difficult for the gardens to be used and

11.6
The design/build projects at the Danny Woo Community Garden focus on common gathering spaces, leaving the garden plots open to individual gardeners' creativity and effort. Photograph by Jeffrey Hou, 2003.

accepted as a neighborhood space. For example, in the case of Thistle P-Patch, a lack of amenities and visual cues reinforced the perception of the garden as a marginal space within the neighborhood. The lack of definable edges, together with the garden's location along a utility corridor, attracted illegal dumping that further entrenched the neighbors' negative perception of the garden. To address this issue, a perimeter fence and attractive gateways were installed. In this regard, Bradner Gardens Park offers an example in which artful structures, sculptures, and ornamental gardens have helped establish an identity for the garden and invite neighbors to use the park.

Striking a balance between permanence and flexibility is a unique challenge in the design of urban community gardens. Given the evolution of gardens over time, a model design is one that provides a useful framework while still encouraging modification and adaptation by the users. The design of Bradner Gardens Park again serves as an example. The park master plan provides a framework that allows for incremental additions and adjustments. The design and construction of the built features in the park are also simple enough for gardeners and users to modify and replicate later, depending on the evolving needs of the community. The result is a park design with a strong visual identity and a sense of place, yet which leaves open possibilities for continued growth and community involvement in future improvements and changes. The Danny Woo Community Garden provides another example in which a framework was established through initial planning to address common access and entries. The design/build projects focus only on built structures, leaving the garden spaces untouched so that gardeners can personalize and define their own plots. This framework allows for incremental adjustments according to the needs of individual gardeners.

Involvement of Professional Designers

Because physical design still plays a critical role in community gardens, professional involvement can be an asset to the development and design of the gardens. In spite of the incremental and ad-hoc nature of design and construction in community gardens, all of the selected case studies from Seattle have received some degree of professional assistance in the form of contracted services or voluntary help. For example, Bradner Gardens Park and Magnuson Community Garden were planned and designed by Barker Landscape Architects, a locally based landscape architecture firm. At Bradner Gardens Park, the park master plan developed by Barker Landscape Architects provided the framework for the design of specific garden elements by other designers, including the Neighborhood Design/Build Studio at the University of Washington. The Danny Woo Community Garden also receives continued support from design faculty and students from the University of Washington. The toolshed/kitchen at Interbay was designed and built by SHED, a local design/build firm. Marra Farm received assistance from Jones and Jones Architects and Landscape Architects in developing a master plan that the coalition then used to leverage funding and resources. The Marra Farm Coalition also received support from two graduate students in architecture from the University of Washington in building a toolshed, and assistance from a landscape architecture graduate student during the farm's master planning process.

In Seattle, the involvement of professionals in the design and building of community gardens has led to the development of a specialized practice for local firms as well as academic design programs. For example, building on the experience and accomplishment of the master planning process at Bradner Gardens Park, Barker Landscape Architects has gone on to develop a track record of projects in planning and designing urban community gardens and community open space, including the Magnuson Community Garden and, more recently, the playfield at Bryant Elementary School in northeast Seattle. In addition to their involvement with Marra Farm, Jones and Jones has had a history of providing service to a number of community-based projects in Seattle, including the Cesar Chavez Park, the Cascade Eco-Renovation project, Mt. Baker Ridge Viewpoint Park, and Oxbow Park—all of which are located in struggling neighborhoods. Jones and Jones' professional involvement has helped to leverage important funding and support in the realization of these projects. Following involvement at Danny Woo Community Garden, Professor Steve Badanes of the University of Washington has developed a design/build curriculum focusing on neighborhood-scale and community-based projects. Badanes' Neighborhood Design/Build Studio has since completed other projects at Bradner Gardens Park and throughout the Seattle area.

The specialized practice of designing urban community gardens and similar types of community open space requires skills and experience in engaging community stakeholders and understanding the community process. This involves working

closely and effectively with neighborhood and community organizations, as well as an appreciation for user-initiated design and the process of place making. At Bradner Gardens Park, the master plan provided a framework for the subsequent development of individual structures that involved additional community input and refinement of the overall design. The master plan did not complete the design but rather allowed for further improvement and improvisation. At the Danny Woo Community Garden, Badanes' design/build studio developed a different process that identified individual built structures to serve specific functions in the garden while leaving the rest of the garden to be continuously built and modified by the gardeners and volunteers. In both cases, meetings and conversations with community stakeholders presented the initial step toward understanding the nature of the projects.

In the selected case studies from Seattle, the involvement of architects, artists, builders, horticulturists, and landscape architects brings a variety

11.8
Gateway at the High Point Market Garden designed and built by the Pomegranate Center. The involvement of professionals can enhance the quality and identity of a garden. Photograph by Arielle Farina Clark, 2005.

11.9
The perimeter fence at the High Point Market Garden resulted from the vision of a community artist, and the contributions of several gardeners, neighbors, and community volunteers. Photograph by Vanessa Lee, 2007.

of skills and expertise to the gardens that are important in supporting the programming and evolution of the gardens. At Bradner Gardens Park, landscape architects developed the initial master plan that provided the framework for the subsequent design and construction of architectural components as well as the creation of ornamental gardens. For the current location of the Interbay P-Patch, a Parks Department landscape architect developed the construction drawings of the gardener-driven design, and an architecture design/build firm collaborated with gardeners to design and construct the garden's landmark shed structure. At Danny Woo Community Garden, landscape architecture students from the University of Washington assisted in an earlier phase to define garden areas and paths, and this work was followed up by the work of architectural studios years later. At Marra Farm, the ongoing development of the site has involved both architecture and landscape architecture students, who provided different services to the design and development of the site.

Community-University Partnership: Community-Based Design Studios

Community-university partnerships have been important to the development of a number of Seattle's community gardens. As a service to local communities, such partnerships bring much-needed resources, volunteer help, and expertise in design and construction. Besides Professor Steve Badanes' Neighborhood Design/Build Studio, Associate Professor Daniel Winterbottom in the University of Washington's Department of Landscape Architecture has also developed an award-winning program in community design/build. His interdisciplinary studio was responsible for the improvement of the University Heights P-Patch, and another studio has undertaken the design and construction of Cascade Park adjacent to the Cascade P-Patch, in addition to a variety of local and international community-based projects. In addition to Steve Badanes and Daniel Winterbottom, faculty in both the architecture and landscape architecture departments at the University of Washington have created other innovative programs that provide learning opportunities for students as well as services to the local communities, particularly those that are underserved. Because programs like these often require less financial resources on the part of the community, they fill an important void created by economic and political gaps among neighborhoods in the city.

Community-university partnerships in the context of urban community gardens provide multiple community and educational benefits. Communities receive volunteer support and technical assistance from the students and faculty. The excitement generated by working together with students often encourages the community to invest more efforts. For design studios, urban community gardens in particular provide a suitable scale to conduct design/builds. By engaging community stakeholders in the design/build process, the experience also exposes the students to the nuances of participatory design and community process. Students learn about the specific

nature of user-initiated design and the organic and incremental process of building. These experiences often compel the students to consider how design and construction techniques must attend to subsequent durability, repair, and maintenance concerns. The community-based experience can also encourage students to become active in serving the local community. In a few cases, students from the studios have stayed involved and become active members of the respective garden community.

Rather than setting up competition, community-university partnerships can complement professional practice by providing much-needed support for local communities and neighborhoods to be able to design and develop community gardens. The experience of Bradner Gardens Park offers an example in which professional landscape architects provided contracted service in developing a master plan that led to and guided the involvement of university design studios and professional architecture firms, as well as horticultural groups, other nonprofit organizations, and city agencies, in implementing the design of the park and its program elements.

HYBRID PUBLIC SPACE

I think the City of Seattle is getting a great deal from P-Patches, because they give up the land, but they're getting a park that's getting taken care of by volunteers. And for the most part, in Seattle parks, you don't get that.
—A GARDENER AT BRADNER GARDENS PARK

Urban community gardens can be best characterized as a form of hybrid public space in the contemporary urban environment that crosses many social, institutional, and disciplinary boundaries. For the most part, urban community gardens in Seattle occupy public properties but are frequently managed by neighborhood activists and volunteers, including individual gardeners. Sometimes community gardens turn private properties into public use, as in the case of Danny Woo Community Garden. As such, they break down the normative boundaries between "public" and "private" domains. In the selected case studies in Seattle, the gardens represent the collective efforts of multiple stakeholders, which include public agencies, nonprofit organizations, informal neighborhood groups, activists, citizens, private businesses, and professionals in planning and design. Because many gardens combine multiple uses that are either necessitated by the limitations of the site or intended to invite multiple users, the multiple uses in turn blur the distinctions between types of public open space and program functions. As an example, the case of Bradner Gardens Park successfully blends active and passive recreation as well as neighborhood spaces and gardening activities. Similarly, Magnuson Community Garden, as a kind of "stroll garden" within a large park, attracts joggers and others. The combination of uses and functions raises the possibility of rethinking the programming and design of public space in contemporary cities.

As hybrid public spaces, community gardens offer opportunities to link institutional support and community activism. In Seattle, institutional mechanisms and support structures have been critical in sustaining the growth of local community gardens. Unlike other cities, where community gardens are often outcomes of isolated efforts by individuals and communities, Seattle's community gardens have been a result of collective efforts and deliberate partnerships between the public sector and civil society. Specifically, entities and mechanisms such as the P-Patch Program, the Neighborhood Matching Fund, and the Memorandum of Agreement with the Parks Department provide key support for the proliferation and maintenance of the numerous community gardens in the city.

The Neighborhood Matching Fund program, developed by the Seattle Department of Neighborhoods under the leadership of its former director, Jim Diers, has provided the institutional mechanism and incentive for such synergistic processes to occur. By linking the level of neighborhood activism and involvement with funding opportunities, the program encourages and motivates neighborhood groups and activists to engage a broader constituency through creative activities. The grants also facilitate the involvement of professionals who are working for the community group rather than the authority. Besides the Seattle Department of Neighborhoods, other local agencies, such as the Seattle Housing Authority and the WSU King County Extension, also provide support for community gardens and urban agriculture through their own programs. Furthermore, a network of nonprofit organizations and community garden advocates, particularly the P-Patch Trust, has played a critical role in offering much-needed technical expertise, educational activities, advocacy, resources, and volunteer help for the community gardens. The presence of these organizations reflects and promotes a strong culture of environmental stewardship and community organizing in the city.

IS SEATTLE UNIQUE?

The support given to community gardens in Seattle may seem unique in many ways. The physical, social, and political environment seems to align in beneficial ways to support community gardens. Because of the mild maritime climate, the gardens in Seattle may stay active and green year round, so they are more likely to be attractive to the nongardening audience. The rich valleys have historically provided good gardening soil, while the steeply sloped hills offer unbuildable sites that can be used for gardening. The engaged civic culture that values neighborhood identity and participation has led to community gardens being promoted as neighborhood amenities and assets, which the political structure supports at multiple levels. Community gardeners in Seattle have access to resources through the city-run P-Patch Program as well as other public agencies and private organizations that assist in their efforts. Funding is available on a competitive basis to community groups seeking to improve neighborhood spaces for the public good, and community garden groups have been very savvy in soliciting these resources.

Seattle is also known as a socially progressive city that actively provides support for underserved populations, including new immigrants and refugees. Community gardens in particular become a venue of support—especially for immigrant and refugee groups who wish to continue their agrarian traditions and find stability in a new environment. The Seattle Housing Authority has embraced community gardens by locating them on their sites to provide the mostly immigrant population with the opportunity to grow food and gain supplemental income through Community Supported Agriculture gardening.

With all of these unique characteristics, are the experiences of community gardens in Seattle replicable in other cities and regions? Can cities and communities with different social, political, and physical contexts emulate the success of the community garden programs in Seattle?

Despite its seemingly unique conditions, Seattle faces challenges that are common to community gardens in other cities. Issues such as impermanent land use, scarce resources, crime and vandalism, and neighborhood changes are everyday challenges among many community gardens. Although there are fewer community gardens in Seattle that rely on leased land, the use of public land is still subject to political change in the city. The reduction in the amount of Neighborhood Matching Funds available is an example of the volatile nature of institutional support in the face of political and economic change. Although the strong environmental and social values in Seattle may be unique, it is also increasingly common to find in other regions similar practices involving sustainable environmental management, reuse of vacant and industrial lands, and building partnerships across institutional and social boundaries. Cities such as Portland, Oregon, and St. Paul, Minnesota, have been pioneers in such efforts (Diers 2004).

While physical factors such as topography and climate are place-specific, many of the features that have contributed to the success of Seattle community gardens are the result of conscious and deliberate efforts carried out over a long period of time. They represent the collective efforts of dedicated individuals and groups. Many of these efforts can be replicated, and some are already being implemented in other cities and regions. For example, the Neighborhood Matching Fund program has been used as a model in many other cities and municipalities, from North America to East Asia and South Africa (Diers 2004). The proliferation of matching grant programs based on the Seattle model is an indication that the Seattle experience can at least be partially replicated and adapted to meet the specific social, institutional, and environmental conditions of other cities. The multiple types of community gardens in Seattle are themselves a manifestation of and response to different contexts, limitations, and opportunities. While the Seattle model is not likely to be entirely replicated and cannot be generalized across different contexts, its experiences offer many lessons for communities, cities, and regions to find their own approaches that meet the needs of different communities and localities.

12

Visions of Urban Community Gardens

PEOPLE, COMMUNITIES, AND CITIES

From fostering anti-poverty programs to neighborhood open space, community gardens have come a long way in becoming a recurring feature of urban landscapes in America. Affording sustainability and community building, economic security, and health, the benefits of community gardens are now more widely recognized and better understood. More individuals and a wider range of programs have been involved in the development and management of urban community gardens. Instead of being simply makeshift spaces, many urban community gardens have become enduring places that involve professional design as well as active community engagement.

In spite of these advances, much more can be done to make community gardens an integral part of neighborhoods, cities, and regions. Specifically, recognition at the city level of the community garden as a legitimate urban land use and open space category is essential in ensuring institutional support for urban community gardens. Active support from neighborhoods and communities also is important in making urban community gardens thriving places in contemporary cities. Given the multiple benefits of community gardens, a greater vision of community gardens for the continuing transformation of the urban environment is needed.

Building on existing trends of community garden programs nationwide and on the case of community gardens in Seattle, this chapter outlines a set of ideas and steps to realize the full potential of community gardens as places that contribute to the sustainability and health of people, communities, and cities.

INDIVIDUALS AND FAMILIES: CHOICES, DIVERSITY, AND EMPOWERMENT

Unlike most other urban open spaces, community gardens involve the direct participation of individuals and families through design, gardening, maintenance, community activities, and celebrations. Distinctly different from large parks and open space that require large capital and extensive bureaucratic process in their development, community gardens provide individuals in the urban context with choices and opportunities to shape and interact with the environment. On an everyday basis, they provide opportunities to grow food and alleviate household expenses. They offer individuals places to exercise and maintain a more active lifestyle. Community gardens involve people from all stages and walks of life. They can engage the affluent and the poor, and those at all levels in between. Through programs and interactions with others, gardens provide opportunities to learn about and inspire involvement in culture, nutrition, and environmental stewardship.

As places that can be constructed and maintained through small collective efforts, community gardens enable individuals to take actions to address issues in neighborhoods and communities. Because community gardens offer such wide-ranging opportunities for the direct participation of a wide variety of individuals, community gardens visions should be based on an enabling approach and an inclusive nature. A welcoming and inclusive community garden should provide people with choices. Community gardens are places where one can garden as a hobby and learn new skills. They are also places where individuals and families can grow food and find mutual support to meet their everyday needs.

To provide choices for the diverse needs of individuals and families and to allow for a variety of activities and actions, community gardens need to be inclusive in their design and management. Differences in values, cultures and garden practices need to be acknowledged and understood. Community gardens can follow multiple models and encourage a mixture of uses depending on individual choices and the needs of a particular context. Designed for choice and diversity, community gardens can empower individuals and families to take action in their larger community and environment. At the individual and family level, choice, diversity, and empowerment should be an integral part of a vision of future urban community gardens.

NEIGHBORHOOD AND COMMUNITY: RECONSTRUCTING THE COMMONS

In addition to offering individual choice and action, community gardens provide a variety of collective benefits to neighborhoods and communities—in both geographical and social terms. They provide places and opportunities for recreation, learning, gathering, and social events for communities that may be defined by geographic boundaries or by social networks. As places of community gathering and collective actions, community gardens can help reconstruct the "social commons"—a shared space at the heart of the community that in recent history has been undermined by the sprawl of low-density single-use development and the privatization of public space (Linn 1999).

However, community gardens are more than just a typical common space. They provide a model for people to interact with a place that is different from other forms of park and open space. Through interactions on the sites and the processes of development and maintenance, community gardens foster deeper connections among members of a community. Through opportunities to participate in various garden activities, including maintenance and management, community gardens can help make neighborhoods and communities become more open and democratic places. By involving neighbors and community members in a variety of tasks, community gardens can also promote social learning and environmental stewardship.

Because community gardens are managed by participants, they can be reshaped and adapted to meet the community's needs, including food production, recreation, social engagement, and more. They also provide a way for people to reclaim and utilize marginal and unused lands that are otherwise vulnerable to misuse. Transformed into community gardens, spaces such as rooftops, sidewalk strips, and vacant lots can become vital community destinations. As places that are built incrementally and through both individual and collective efforts, community gardens provide opportunities for the negotiation of interests, values, and identities. As cities become increasingly multicultural, community gardens provide opportunities for different cultural groups to interact. By providing multiple social, economic, and health benefits, community gardens present a new model of the "neighborhood common" that should be considered a part of the neighborhood infrastructure, similar to the basic necessity of neighborhood parks, playgrounds, community centers, schools, and libraries.

DISTRICTS, CITIES, AND COALITION: FROM ISLANDS TO NETWORKS

Most urban gardens in cities today are small in scale. They tend to occupy vacant lands and residual urban spaces that are often fragmented and isolated. But because of their adaptability and flexibility, as well as their ability to activate unused and marginal lands, community gardens have the potential to become part of a larger network of open space in the urban landscape. With minimal infrastructure investment, community gardens provide a cost-effective strategy to recover unused and marginal urban lands and turn them into valuable assets. Specifically, with the ability to activate a range of urban sites, community gardens can play a critical role in connecting previously disparate urban lands at the district and city levels and turning them into functional corridors for people and wildlife. Since these marginal and unused lands tend to be located along transportation routes, utility easements,

12.1
Danny Woo Community Garden is an example of reclaiming urban landscape and making communities and the city more livable and sustainable. Photograph by Leslie Gia Clark, 2007.

waterfronts, and other linear corridors, there is great potential to transform these corridors into multifunctional networks. These corridors can incorporate other program elements to serve different users, as well as urban ecological functions such as filtration and storage of storm-water runoff. Similarly, these corridors could connect varied civic facilities, such as schools, libraries, and community centers, whose educational functions can be conceptually and programmatically linked with the gardens.

The gardens themselves need not be literally continuous. They can be connected by trails, paths, and pedestrian-friendly streets and sidewalks. When gardens connect to other civic amenities and residential neighborhoods by pedestrian and bike paths, there is an increased likelihood to reduce car trips—another environmental and social benefit. Having community gardens along trails and paths can help increase the use of those existing networks. Once connected through such networks, community gardens provide benefits not only to individual gardeners and neighborhoods but also to the broader public by enhancing the access and quality of green open spaces for all.

Having community gardens as a network and alliance that is supported by other kinds of social and physical connections increases the capacity and outcomes of the gardens. Through a network of sites, organizations and actors can provide better coordination in programming, land-use planning, and policy making, as well as distribution of resources. As issues of climate change, sustainability, food security, environmental social justice, and local economic development become more important, the coalitions of people and networks of resources can support not only the development and management of community gardens but also address broader issues facing districts, cities, and even bioregions.

REALIZING THE VISIONS

The realization of such visions of urban community gardens requires the involvement of a wide range of individuals, organizations, and sources of support that reflect the multiple purposes and roles of the gardens. To move forward, a series of necessary actions is outlined below. The lists of actions are not meant to be exhaustive, since situations and circumstances may call for different types of actions. Rather, they provide a springboard for more specific approaches and efforts.

WHAT GARDENERS CAN DO

- **State their needs.** Gardeners should make their needs known to policy makers, community organizers/leaders, and nongardeners in their community. They should explain to others how they use the gardens and what gardening means to them.
- **Form inclusive task forces or groups to take actions.** As proactive constituents, gardeners should mobilize and undertake initiatives to secure, develop, and build the gardens. They need to garner broader support, through an inclusive process of organizing, designing, developing, and managing the gardens.
- **Take responsibility.** Once a garden has been developed, gardeners should take their share of responsibility in making the garden a functioning and welcoming place for the community.

WHAT DESIGNERS AND PLANNERS CAN DO

- **Learn from gardens and communities.** To become effective agents for neighborhoods and communities, designers and planners need to understand the nature of community gardens and the needs of gardeners.
- **Articulate and advocate.** Because of their specialized knowledge and roles in the planning and development process, design and planning professionals are in a unique position to articulate the needs of community gardens and serve

as advocates for gardeners, neighborhoods, and communities. Furthermore, designers and planners should seek new and creative opportunities for the development of community gardens, even in unlikely places.

- **Interact and engage.** Rather than prescribing solutions and dictating the outcomes, design and planning professionals should seek to interact and engage the garden stakeholders—including gardeners, residents, agency staffs, and community organizers—to collectively develop ideas and solutions.

- **Develop frameworks for incremental development.** To allow gardens to adapt to the changing needs of gardeners and to engage gardeners and community members in the continued evolution of the place rather than completely defining the garden's design, design and planning professionals should focus their efforts in creating an open framework that affords incremental development and adaptation to the garden.

- **Bring social, professional, and financial networks.** Design and planning professionals can bring resources and networks that lie outside the gardens, including technical expertise in construction, connections to different funding sources, and sources of volunteers.

- **Share specialized knowledge.** To ensure that the gardeners can assume the responsibility of continuing to manage and develop the gardens, design and planning professionals have the responsibility of sharing their specialized knowledge in a way that is accessible and useful to the garden stakeholders.

WHAT RESEARCHERS AND EDUCATORS CAN DO

- **Research support mechanisms.** By analyzing lessons from different communities and cities, researchers can devise strategies and suggestions for improving the support mechanisms for urban community gardens that include funding sources.

- **Assist policy decisions.** By documenting the status of the community gardens as well as their challenges and accomplishments, researchers can provide the needed information to assistant communities and cities in making decisions concerning community gardens.

- **Engage students and communities.** University faculty in particular can bring their students to work with the local communities. Community-university partnerships can provide much-needed resources for communities as well as learning opportunities for students.

WHAT NONPROFIT ORGANIZATIONS CAN DO

- **Provide support and assistance.** Nonprofit organizations can play unique and important roles to individual garden groups and garden networks. Some important skills that can be shared include assistance in identifying and soliciting funding support, education about sustainable gardening practices, community development, legal processes, cross-cultural competency, and language assistance.

- **Pool resources.** One of the most important ways that nonprofit organizations can support individual gardens is by pooling together disparate resources. This may include funding, volunteers, and material supplies, as well as technical assistance and educational outreach.
- **Voice and advocate.** Nonprofit organizations can provide a collective voice for a network of community gardens. As collective entities, they play a distinctive role in translating individual needs and issues into broader concerns throughout a larger geographical area.

WHAT CITY OFFICIALS AND AGENCIES CAN DO

- **Provide secured funding and land use.** Public officials and agencies are in a unique and powerful position to secure funding and legitimize permanent land use for urban community gardens—two of the key elements in sustaining a community garden.
- **Establish citywide policies and perspective.** Public officials and agencies set citywide policies and establish frameworks and guidelines from a citywide perspective that are supportive of community gardens. City officials and agencies have a responsibility to ensure equitable distribution of resources to different sectors of the city, especially those that are underserved.
- **Create inclusive citywide open space plans.** City agencies should collaborate to create an interconnected network of open space types, to identify potential co-location of recreational and learning facilities with community gardens to build from synergies of interests and activity, and to identify opportunities for community gardens at varied scales and qualities within this open-space network.
- **Involve stakeholders in the process.** To ensure that the citywide policy and framework meets the needs of gardeners, citizens, and communities, city officials and agencies should commit to processes that actively involve all stakeholders in policy making and oversight, accommodating multiple language groups and those with special needs.
- **Offer community incentives and education.** Rather than simply giving out support, city officials and agencies are in a rare position to create a system of resource distribution based on matching funds/labor and incentives that encourage community initiatives and mobilization. Similarly, city agencies should include staff who provide individuals and groups with assistance and education in undertaking effective outreach and the community organizing necessary for establishing community gardens.

WHAT CITIZENS CAN DO

- **Become a gardener.** Although one does not need to garden to benefit from the community gardens, the most direct way for citizens and community members to support and learn about community gardens is to become a gardener. The greater the demand for garden plots, the more the justification for resources to sustain community gardens.

- **Bring diverse skills and expertise.** Planning, developing, maintaining, managing, and advocating for community gardens requires a broad range of skills and expertise. Although community gardens may involve mostly gardeners, non-gardeners can also play a role. Designers, builders, artists, lawyers, accountants, and others can play important roles in planning and creating a sense of place in community gardens.

- **Engage in multiple levels of involvement.** Citizens can contribute to community gardens at multiple levels. They can volunteer for regular maintenance and improvement of the gardens. They can participate in social events. They may also engage at the policy and planning level by working with community garden advocates and by participating in the public process concerning neighborhood- and city-level planning.

- **Oversee and evaluate.** To ensure that public agencies attend to their responsibilities, citizens can form groups and participate in the public process that oversees and evaluates the implementation of policies and the operation of garden-related programs.

As these actions indicate, making and nurturing community gardens requires active involvement of multiple players over time. The active involvement of these individuals and organizations is important for community gardens to thrive as meaningful places that cultivate enduring personal, civic, and environmental assets. These assets have important implications for the sustainability of our society at all scales: individual and family, neighborhood and community, and district, city, and region. Urban community gardens are therefore as much about gardening as about growing communities and greening cities.

REFERENCES

Abi-Nader, Jeanette, David Buckley, Kendall Dunnigan, and Kristin Markley. 2001. Growing communities curriculum: Community building and organizational development through community gardening. Philadelphia: American Community Gardening Association.

American Community Gardening Association. 1998. American community gardening survey. Monograph. Philadelphia: American Community Gardening Association.

Ammons, David. 1975. State asked to set aside land for "inflation gardens." *Seattle Times*. December 12, A1.

Anderson, Ross, and Sara Jean Green. 2001. A culture slips away. *Seattle Times*. May 27. http://seattletimes.nwsource.com/news/local/seattle_history/articles/story1.html (accessed May 11, 2006).

Aponte-Pares, Luis. 1996. Casitas: Place and culture: Appropriating place in Puerto Rican Barrios. *Places* 11 (1): 54–61.

Aquino-Ramirez, Gloria Beatriz. 1995. Social and nutritional benefits of community gardens for Hispanic-Americans in New York City and Los Angeles. Unpublished thesis, Department of Horticulture, Forestry and Recreation, Kansas State University.

Balmori, Dianne, and Margaret Morton. 1993. *Transitory gardens, uprooted lives.* New Haven: Yale University Press.

Bassett, Thomas. 1981. Reaping the margins: A century of community gardening in America. *Landscape Journal* 25 (2): 1–8.

Blair, Dorothy, Carol Giesecke, and Sandra Sherman. 1991. A dietary, social, and economic evaluation of the Philadelphia Urban Garden Project. *Journal of Nutrition Education* 23 (4): 161–67.

Bloom, Brett, and Ava Bromberg, eds. 2004. *Belltown paradise: The Belltown P-Patch,*
cottage park, growing Vine Street, Buster Simpson. Chicago: White Walls.

Bonham, J. Blaine, Gerri Spilka, and Darl Rastorfer. 2002. *Old cities/green cities: Communities transform unmanaged land.* Planning Advisory Service Report Number 506/507. Chicago: American Planning Association.

Borba, Holly. 1994. City P-Patches help feed low income residents. *Washington Free Press* (August/September). http://www.washingtonfreepress.org/11/P_Patch.html (accessed August 15, 2005).

Boston Urban Gardeners. 1982. *A handbook of community gardening*. Edited by Susan Naimark. New York: Charles Scribner's Sons.

Breslav, Mark. 1991. The common ground of green words. *Community Greening Review* 1 (1): 4–9.

Coe, Mary. 1978. *Growing with community gardening*. Taftsville, Vermont: The Countryman Press.

Cohen, Ellen. 1986. A look at city soil. *Organic Gardening* 33 (4): 102–4, 106–9.

Cooper Marcus, Clare, and Marni Barnes, eds. 1999. Introduction to *Healing gardens: therapeutic benefits and design recommendations*. New York: John Wiley & Sons, Inc.

Corbett, Judy, and Michael Corbett. 2000. *Designing sustainable communities: Learning from Village Homes*. Washington, D.C.: Island Press.

Cranz, Galen. 1989. *The politics of park design*. Cambridge, MA: MIT Press.

Crowley, Walt. 1999. Pike Place Market (Seattle) thumbnail history. HistoryLink Essay #1602. http://www.historylink.org/essays/printer_friendly/index.cfm?file_id=1602 (accessed May 27, 2006).

Cultivating Communities. N.d. Cultivating communities: A collaborative program of the P-Patch Trust and the P-Patch Program. Seattle: P-Patch Trust and City of Seattle Department of Neighborhoods.

Diers, Jim. 2004. *Neighbor power: Building community the Seattle way*. Seattle: University of Washington Press.

El Centro de la Raza. N.d. Brochure. PDF download from http://www.elcentrodelaraza.com/aboutus/factsheet.htm (accessed March 26, 2009).

Elliott, Carl, and Rob Peterson. 2000. *The maritime northwest garden guide*. Seattle: Seattle Tilth.

Engle, Schuyler. 1992. Urban Farmers. *Seattle Weekly*. September 16, 31-33.

Eskenazi, Stuart. 2001. Familiar landscape lured Scandinavians. *Seattle Times*. November 4. http://www.seattletimes.nwsource.com/news/local/seattle_history/articles/scandinavians.html (accessed May 11, 2006).

Fox, Tom, Ian Koeppel, and Susan Kellam. 1985. *Struggle for space: The greening of New York City, 1970–1984*. New York: Neighborhood Space Coalition.

Francis, Mark. 1987. Some different meanings attached to a city park and community gardens. *Landscape Journal* 6 (2): 101–12.

———. 1999. *Case study method for landscape architecture*. Washington, D.C.: Landscape Architecture Foundation.

———. 2003. *Village Homes: A community by design*. Washington, D.C.: Island Press.

Francis, Mark, Lisa Cashdan, and Lynn Paxson. 1984. *Community open spaces: Greening neighborhoods through community action and land conservation*. Washington, D.C.: Island Press.

Francis, Mark, and Randolph T. Hester, Jr., eds. 1990. *The meaning of gardens : Idea, place, and action*. Cambridge, MA: MIT Press.

Gardens for All. 1973. *Gardens for all: Guide to a greener, happier community.* Charlotte, Vermont: Gardens for All.

Glover, Troy D. 2003. The story of the Queen Anne Memorial Garden: Resisting a dominant cultural narrative. *Journal of Leisure Research* 35 (2): 190–212.

———. 2004. Social capital in the lived experiences of community gardeners. *Leisure Studies* 26: 143–62.

Glover, Troy D., Kimberly Shinew, and Diana Parry. 2005. Association, sociability, and civic culture: The democratic effect of community gardening. *Leisure Sciences* 27: 75–92.

Halverson, Beret, and Jim Flint. 2005. *Patchwork: Stories of gardens and community in Burlington, Vermont.* Burlington, VT: Friends of Burlington Gardens.

Hamm, M. W., and A. C. Bellows. 2003. Community food security and nutrition education. *Journal of Nutrition Education and Behavior* 35 (1): 37–43.

Hassan Loyan, Bashir Nur. 1995. Educational models for community garden programs in the United States and their potential application for Sub-Saharan Africa. Dissertation, Department of Horticulture, Forestry and Recreation, Kansas State University.

Hester, Randolph T. 1984. *Planning neighborhood space with people.* New York: Van Nostrand Reinhold.

———. 2007. *Design for ecological democracy.* Cambridge, MA: MIT Press.

Hough, Michael. 1984. *City form and natural process: Towards a new urban vernacular.* New York: Van Nostrand Reinhold.

Hynes, Patricia. 1996. *A patch of Eden: America's inner-city gardeners.* White River Junction, Vermont: Chelsea Green Publishing Co.

Jamison, Michael S. 1985. The joys of gardening: Collectivist and bureaucratic cultures in conflict. *Sociological Quarterly* 26 (4): 473–90.

Jensen, Jim. 1988. What's doing in the P-Patch? The rebirth of a great community garden. *National Gardening* 11 (8): 280–89, 56–57.

Jobb, Jamie. 1979. *The complete book of community gardening.* New York: William Morrow and Company, Inc.

Johnson, Lorraine. 2005. Design for food: landscape architects find roles in city farms. *Landscape Architecture* (June): 30–37.

Kaplan, Rachel. 1973. Some psychological benefits of gardening. *Environment and Behavior* 5: 143–62.

———. 1983. The role of nature in the urban context. In *Behavior and the Natural Environment.* Vol. 6 of *Human Behavior and Environment.* Edited by Irwin Altman and Joachim Wohlwill. New York: Plenum Press.

Kirschbaum, Pamela R. 2000. Making policy in a crowded world: Steps beyond the physical garden. *Community Greening Review* 10: 2–11.

Kruckeberg, Arthur R. 2003. *The Natural History of Puget Sound Country.* Seattle: University of Washington Press.

Kueter, Vince. 2001. Seattle through the years. *Seattle Times,* November 13. http://

seattletimes.nwsource.com/news/local/seattle_history/articles/timeline.html (accessed May 11, 2006).

Landman, Ruth H. 1993. *Creating community in the city: Cooperatives and community gardens in Washington, D.C.* Westport, CT: Bergin and Garvey.

Lawson, Laura. 2004. The planner in the garden: A historical view into the relationship between planning and community gardens. *Journal of Planning History* 3 (2): 151–76.

———. 2005. *City bountiful: A century of community gardening in America.* Berkeley: University of California Press.

Lawson, Laura, and Marcia McNally. 1995. Putting teens at the center: Maximizing public utility of urban open space through youth involvement in planning and empowerment. *Children's Environments* 12 (2): 209-21.

Leonard, Lewis Y. 1934. Memorandum to Macennis Moore, dated April 25. Subject: News Copy on County Garden of Seattle. Washington State Archives, 1933–1937. Record Group 55.

Lettuce Link. 2006/2007. *Lettuce Ink* 2 (3). http://www.solid-ground.org/Programs/Nutrition/Lettuce/Documents/LL2Q.pdf (accessed October 25, 2007).

Lewis, Charles. 1979. Healing in the urban environment: A person/plant viewpoint. *Journal of the American Planning Association* 45: 330–38.

———. 1996. *Green nature/human nature: The meaning of plants in our lives.* Chicago: University of Illinois Press.

Librizzi, Lenny. 1999. Comprehensive Plans, Zoning Regulations, Open Space Policies and Goals Concerning Community Gardens and Open Green Space from the Cities of Seattle, Berkeley, Boston and Chicago. For GreenThumb Grow Together Workshop "Lessons From Community Gardening Programs In Other Cities," March 20, 1999.

Linn, Karl. 1991. *From rubble to restoration: Sustainable habitats through urban agriculture.* San Francisco: Urban Habitat Program of the Earth Island Institute.

———. 1999. Reclaiming the sacred commons. *New Village* 1 (1): 42–49.

Macdonald, Rich. 2006. E-mail correspondence. September 20.

Malakoff, David. 1994. Final harvest? *Community Greening Review* 4: 4–12.

McRoberts, Patrick. 1999. King county voters on forward thrust bonds approve stadium and aquarium and nix transit on February 13, 1968. HistoryLink Essay #2168. http://www.historylink.org/essays/output.cfm?file_id=2168 (accessed May 27, 2006).

McRoberts, Patrick, and Kit Oldham. 2003. Fort Lawton military police clash with Native American and other protesters in the future Discovery Park on March 8, 1970. HistoryLink Essay # 5513. http://www.historylink.org/essays/printer_friendly/index.cfm?file_id=5513 (accessed May 27, 2006).

Monroe-Santos, Suzanne. 1997. Longevity in urban community gardens. Master's thesis, Science in International Agriculture, University of California, Davis.

Moore, Bibby. 1989. *Growing with gardening: A twelve-month guide for therapy, recreation, and education*. Chapel Hill: University of North Carolina Press.

Parry, Diana C., Troy D. Glover, and Kimberly J. Shinew. 2005. 'Mary, Mary quite contrary, how does your garden grow?' Examining gender roles and relations in community gardens. *Leisure Studies* 24 (2): 177–92.

Patel, Ishwarbhai C. 1991. Gardening's socioeconomic impacts: Community gardening in an urban setting. *Journal of Extension* 29 (Winter): 7–8.

PCC Natural Markets. 2006. PCC history. http://www.pccnaturalmarkets.com/about/history.html (accessed May 28, 2006).

Pierce, Donna, Eileen Eininger, Nancy Allen, and Barbara Donnette. 1995. *The city gardener's cookbook: Totally fresh, mostly vegetarian, decidedly delicious recipes from Seattle's P-Patches*. Seattle: Sasquatch Books.

Pothukuchi, Kameshwari. 2004. Community food assessment: A first step in planning for community food security. *Journal of Planning Education and Research* 23: 356–77.

Pothukuchi, Kameshwari, and Jerome L. Kaufman. 2000. The food system: A stranger to the planning field. *APA Journal* 66 (2): 113–24.

P-Patch Trust. 2004. Annual report. http://www.ppatchtrust.org/2004_annual_report.doc (accessed October 30, 2007).

———. 2006. History. http://www.ppatchtrust.org/About.html (accessed May 10, 2006).

Project for Public Spaces. 2000. *Public parks, private partners.* New York: Project for Public Spaces.

Rea, Dave. 1973. P-Party: Vegetarianism reigns as city officials dine. *Seattle Times* (August 25): A4.

Relf, Dianne. 1979. Therapy through horticulture. *Brooklyn Botanical Garden Record/Plants and Gardens* 35 (1): 18–19.

Santos, Bob. 2002. *Hum bows, not hot dogs! Memoirs of a savvy Asian American activist.* Seattle: International Examiner Press.

Saxe, Genevieve. 1936. Report of the Garden and Food Preservation Program in the State of Washington for the 1936 season. Olympia, Washington: State of Washington Department of Social Security.

Schmelzkopf, Karen. 1995. Urban community gardens as contested spaces. *Geographical Review* 85 (3): 364–80.

Schukoske, Jane E. 2000. Community development through gardening: State and local policies transforming urban open space. *New York University Journal of Legislation and Public Policy* 3: 351–61.

Seattle (City of) Department of Neighborhoods. 2006a. P-Patch community gardens starting a new P-Patch. http://www.seattle.gov/neighborhoods/ppatch/start.htm (accessed May 10, 2006).

———. 2006b. P-patch community gardens cultivating communities. http://www.seattle.gov/neighborhoods/ppatch/cultivating.htm (accessed May 10, 2006).

———. 2006c. Neighborhood matching fund. http://www.seattle.gov/neighborhoods/nmf/about.htm (accessed November 7, 2006).

———. 2006d. Neighborhood matching fund. Small and Simple Projects Fund. http://www.seattle.gov/neighborhoods/nmf/smallandsimple.htm (accessed May 28, 2006).

———. 2006e. Neighborhood matching fund. Large Projects Fund. http://www.seattle.gov/neighborhoods/nmf/largeproject.htm (accessed May 28, 2006).

———. 2007. P-Patch community gardening program. http://www.seattle.gov/neighborhoods/ppatch/gardening.htm (accessed November 1, 2007).

Seattle (City of) Department of Planning and Development. 2003a. Demographic snapshots: Seattle's overall poverty rate declined in the 1990s. Excerpted from November 2003 issue of *dpdINFO*. http://www.seattle.gov/dclu/demographics/glance/asp (accessed May 11, 2006).

———. 2003b. Demographic snapshots: Seattle poverty rates vary widely. Excerpted from December 2003 issue of *dpdINFO*. http://www.seattle.gov/dclu/demographics/glance/asp (accessed May 11, 2006).

Seattle (City of) Legislative Information Service. 2008. Resolution Number 30194. City of Seattle Legislative Information Service. http://clerk.ci.seattle.wa.us/~scripts/nph-brs.exe?s1=&s2=&s3=30194&s4=&Sect4=AND&l=20&Sect1=IMAGE&Sect2=THESON&Sect3=PLURON&Sect5=RESN1&Sect6=HITOFF&d=RESN&p=1&u=%2F%7Epublic%2Fresn1.htm&r=1&f=G (updated as of April 14, 2008; accessed April 14, 2008).

Seattle (City of) Office of Intergovernmental Relations. 2006. The greater Seattle data sheet.

Seattle (City of) Parks and Recreation Department. 2005. Pro parks levy opportunity fund. City of Seattle. http://www.seattle.gov/proparks/opportunityfund.htm (updated September 28, 2006; accessed May 29, 2006).

———. 2006. Pro parks levy history. http://www.seattle.gov/proparks/history.htm (updated May 10, 2006; accessed May 28, 2006).

———. 2007a. Pro parks levy overall summary. http://www.seattle.gov/parks/proparks/levyinfo.htm (updated June 7, 2007; accessed November 1, 2007).

———. 2007b. Pro parks a-z project list. http://www.seattle.gov/parks/ProParks/projects.htm (updated October 24, 2007; accessed November 2, 2007).

Seattle Tilth. 2007. Demonstration gardens. http://www.seattletilth.org/resources/demonstrationgardens (accessed November, 1, 2007).

Seattle Times. 1974. Okay given to buy original P-Patch. December 4, A4.

Smith, Deborah J. 1998. Horticultural therapy: The garden benefits everyone. *Journal of Psychosocial Nursing and Mental Health* 36 (10): 14–21.

Solid Ground. 2007. Lettuce Link. http://www.solid-ground.org/Programs/Nutrition/Lettuce/Pages/default.aspx (accessed November 1, 2007).

Sommers, Larry. 1984. *The community garden book.* Burlington: Gardens for All.

Spirn, Anne Whiston. 1984 *Granite garden: Urban nature and human design.* New York: Basic Books.

————. 1998. *Language of landscape.* New Haven: Yale University Press.

Thorne, Judy. 1983. Seattle's Popular P-Patch Program is in trouble. *Seattle Times.* June 28, C1.

Trelstad, Brian. 1997. Little machines and their gardens: A history of school gardens in America. *Landscape Journal* 16 (2): 161–73.

Trust for Public Land. 1995. Cluster report for Bay Area urban farms and gardens. Prepared by Nadine Golden, Arlene Rodriguez, and Laura Lawson. San Francisco: Trust for Public Land.

Ulrich, Roger. 1984. View through a window may influence recovery from surgery. *Science* 224 (April 27): 420–22.

Ulrich, Roger S. 1999. Effects of gardens on health outcomes: Theory and research. In *Healing Gardens: Therapeutic Benefits and Design Recommendations.* Edited by Clare Cooper Marcus and Marni Barnes. New York: John Wiley & Sons, Inc.

United States Census Bureau. 2000. www.census.gov (accessed October 29, 2007).

Warner, Sam Bass 1987. *To dwell is to garden.* Boston: Northeastern University Press.

Washington State University (WSU) King County Extension. 2006. Master Gardener program. http://king.wsu.edu/reports/documents/MG.pdf, dated June 2006 (accessed November 2, 2007).

————. 2007a. Master Gardeners. http://king.wsu.edu/gardening/mastergardener. htm (accessed November 1, 2007).

————. 2007b. Food Sense CHANGE. http://king.wsu.edu/nutrition/change.htm (updated October 30, 2007; accessed November 15, 2007).

Watson, Kenneth Greg. 2003. Seattle, Chief Noah. HistoryLink.org Essay 5071. http://www.historylink.org/essays/loutput.cfm?file_id=5071 (accessed November 1, 2007).

Whitebear, Bernie. 1994. A brief history of the United Indians of all tribes foundation. http://www.unitedindians.org/about_history_bernie.html (accessed October 30, 2007).

Wilma, David. 2000. Chicano activists occupy abandoned school that becomes El Centro on October 11, 1972. HistoryLink.org Essay 2588. http://www.historylink. org/essays/printer_friendly/index.cfm?file_id=2588 (accessed May 27, 2006).

Winterbottom, Daniel. 1998. Casitas: Gardens of reclamation. Environmental Design Research Association Conference Proceedings. April 1998.

REFERENCES AND SOURCES FOR SPECIFIC CASE STUDIES

Interbay References

Alexander, Gemma. 2004. Solar energy fuels imagination and innovation of Interbay gardeners. *P-Patch Post* (Spring): 4. Seattle: P-Patch Trust.

Cropp, Mary. 2005. Ballard high students grow starts for Interbay food bank garden. *P-Patch Post* (Summer): 4. Seattle: P-Patch Trust.

Deneen, Sally. 2000. Cultivating community. *Organic Gardening* 47 (5): 34–42.

Hucka, Judy. 2002. Deb Rock: Food bank coordinator extraordinaire. *P-Patch Post.* (Fall): 3. Seattle: Friends of P-Patch.

Lovejoy, Anne. 2004. P-Patch's generosity in full bloom after 30 years. *Seattle Post Intelligencer.* August 19.

Macdonald, Rich. 2004a. News from other P-Patch gardens. *P-Patch Post* (Fall): 4. Seattle: P-Patch Trust.

———. 2004b. News From other P-Patch gardens. *P-Patch Post* (Winter): 5. Seattle: P-Patch Trust.

Rowley, Jon. 1998. Interbay "Celebrity Compost." *P-Patch Post* (Winter): 5. Seattle: Friends of P-Patch.

———. 1999. Interbay mulch. *P-Patch Post.* (Fall): 2. Seattle: Friends of P-Patch.

———. 2002. Seattle's million flower compost helps restore New York community garden. *Seattle Neighborhood News* 12 (3): 1-2. Seattle: City of Seattle Department of Neighborhoods.

Saul, Kathleen Triesch. 2000. Green acre P-Patches provide ordinary citizens the opportunity to grow their own produce while enjoying the camaraderie of others. *Seattle Times* (July 19): F1, F4.

Schutte, Ray. 1997a. Interbay update. *P-Patch Post* (Summer): 9. Seattle: Friends of P-Patch.

———. 1997b. News from Interbay. *P-Patch Post* (Fall): 9. Seattle: Friends of P-Patch.

———. 1999a. From Interbay. *P-Patch Post* (Summer): 10. Seattle: Friends of P-Patch.

———. 1999b. Interbay gardening notes. *P-Patch Post* (Fall): 5. Seattle: Friends of P-Patch.

Schutte, Ray, and Sean Phelan. 2000. South East Asian soil building. *P-Patch Post* (Fall): 2. Seattle: Friends of P-Patch.

Seattle (City of) Department of Neighborhoods. 2005. P-patch community gardens Interbay. http://www.ci.seattle.wa.us/neighborhoods/ppatch/locations/11.htm (accessed June 10, 2005).

Seattle (City of) Legislative Information Service. 2008. Resolution Number 29459. http://clerk.ci.seattle.wa.us/~scripts/nph-brs.exe?s1=&s2=&s3=29459&s4=&Sect4=AND&l=20&Sect2=THESON&Sect3=PLURON&Sect5=RESN1&Sect6=HITOFF&d=RESN&p=1&u=%2F%7Epublic%2Fresn1.htm&r=1&f=G (updated as of April 23, 2008; accessed April 23, 2008).

Seattle Post-Intelligencer. 2006a. Queen Anne Census Data. http://seattlepi.nwsource.com/webtowns/census.asp?WTID=11 (accessed May 11, 2006).

———. 2006b. Magnolia Census Data. http://seattlepi.nwsource.com/webtowns/census.asp?WTID=8 (accessed May 11, 2006).

Sexton, Mary. 2001. Interbay. *P-Patch Post* (Spring): 4. Seattle: Friends of P-Patch.

Swee, Bruce. 2000. To catch a thief. *P-Patch Post* (Summer). Seattle: Friends of P-Patch.

———, publisher. 2005. Interbay P-Patch 2005 gardeners' handbook.

Swee, Chris. 2003. Interbay finishes new shed. *P-Patch Post.* (Spring): 4. Seattle: Friends of P-Patch.

Thorness, Bill. 2002. Delivering symbolic compost to a rebuilt New York garden. *P-Patch Post* (Winter): 1. Seattle: Friends of P-Patch.

Thistle P-Patch References

Chao, Yao Fou. 1997. Thistle. *P-Patch Post* (Spring): 8. Seattle: Friends of P-Patch.

Higgins, Mark. N.d. Problems linger but there are signs of hope. *Seattle Post-Intelligencers.* http://seattlepi.nwsource.com/neighbors/rainiervalley/hood11a.html (accessed February 28, 2006).

Macdonald, Colin. 2004. Tending P-Patch yields food for table and soul. *Seattle Post-Intelligencer* (August 11).

Macdonald, Rich. 2002. News from the P-Patches. *P-Patch Post* (Winter): 6. Seattle Friends of P-Patch.

Seattle (City of) Department of Neighborhoods. 2008. "P-Patch Community Gardens." http://www.ci.seattle.wa.us/neighborhoods/ppatch/locations/18.htm (accessed March 5, 2008).]

Seattle Post-Intelligencer. 2006. Rainier Valley. http://seattlepi.nwsource.com/webtowns/census.asp?WTID=15 (accessed May 11, 2006).

Snel, Alan. 1999. Some fear Rainier Valley change. *Seattle Post-Intelligencer* (August 27).

Washington State University (WSU) King County Extension. 2006. http://www.metrokc.gov/dchs/csd/wsu-ce/ (accessed February 28, 2006).

Danny Woo References

Ching, Doug. 2001. *Seattle's International District: The making of a Pan-Asian American community.* Seattle: International Examiner Press.

Diers, Jim. 2004. *Neighbor power: Building community the Seattle way.* Seattle: University of Washington Press.

Hou, Jeffrey. 2005. Speaking images: A case of photovoice application in community design. Paper presented at Visualizing Change: The Association for Community Design 2005 Annual Conference. New York, March 30–April 1, 2005.

Inter*Im Community Development Association (ICDA). 2006. *The Friends of the Danny Woo Community Garden Newsletter Online.* http://www.interimicda.org/DWGardensOnline.htm (accessed November 7, 2006).

———.2005. http://www.interimicda.org (accessed August 3, 2005).

Palleroni, Sergio. 2004. *Studio at large: Architecture in the service of global communities.* Seattle: University of Washington Press.

Santos, Bob. 2002. *Hum bows, not hot dogs! Memoirs of a savvy Asian American activist.* Seattle: International Examiner Press.

Seattle Post-Intelligencer. 2006. International District Census Data. http://seattlepi.nwsource.com/webtowns/census.asp?WTID=6 (accessed May 11, 2006).

Stratten, Danny. 2001. A jewel in the heart of the city. *P-Patch Post* (Winter): 5. Seattle: Friends of P-Patch.

Bradner Gardens Park References

Diers, Jim. 2004. *Neighbor Power: building community the Seattle way.* Seattle: University of Washington Press.

Easton, Valerie. 2005. On common ground: Seattle gardeners build community, one plot at a time. *Pacific Northwest: Seattle Times Magazine* (February 6).

Friends of Bradner Gardens Park (FBGP). 2006. http://www.nwlink.com/~jmoty/ (accessed January 19, 2006).

Moty, Joyce. 1999. In praise of public spaces. *P-Patch Post* (Fall): 3. Seattle: Friends of P-Patch.

———. 2003. Bradner renovates utility building. *P-Patch Post* (Spring): 5. Seattle: Friends of P-Patch.

Palleroni, Sergio. 2004. *Studio at large: Architecture in the service of global communities.* Seattle: University of Washington Press.

Seattle (City of) Department of Neighborhoods. 2008. Bradner Gardens Park. http://www.ci.seattle.wa.us/neighborhoods/ppatch/locations/22.htm (accessed March 5, 2008).

Seattle (City of) Department of Parks and Recreation. 2006. Bradner Gardens Park. http://www.cityofseattle.net/parks/parkspaces/bradnergardens.htm (accessed January 19, 2006).

Seattle Post-Intelligencer. 2006. Mount Baker Census Data. http://seattlepi.nwsource.com/webtowns/census.asp?WTID=14 (accessed May 11, 2006).

Seattle Public Utilities (SPU). 2006. About ecoturf. http://www.ci.seattle.wa.us/util/Services/Yard/Natural_Lawn_&_Garden_Care/Natural_Lawn_Care/ABOUT-ECOT_200311261654594.asp (accessed January 19, 2006).

Marra Farm References

Alexander, Gemma. 2003. Weeds got your goat: Goats get the weeds in Marra Farm experiment. *P-Patch Post* (Winter): 3. Seattle: Friends of P-Patch.

American Institute of Architects (AIA) Seattle. 2006. "The architecture of community: Learning from South Park." http://www.aiaseattle.org/event_060127_southpark.htm (accessed April 6, 2006).

Chansanchai, Athima. 2005. Marra Farm plants seeds for South Park community. *Seattle Post Intelligence*r (June 3). http://seattlepi.nwsource.com (accessed June 13, 2005).

Concord Elementary School. 2005. Concord Elementary School 2005 annual report. Seattle: Seattle Public Schools.

Davis, Rachel. 2006. Fertile Ground Youth find roots in South Park garden. *Real Change News.Org* (March 23). http://www.realchangenews.org/2006/2006_03_22/fetileground.html (accessed April 6, 2006).

Fremont Public Association. 2005. http://www.fremontpublic.org/client/morem-arra3.html (accessed August 15, 2005).

Haizlip, Mark F., and Greg R. Squires. 2005. *The Marra Farm community classroom.* Master's Thesis, Department of Architecture, University of Washington.

Harper, Lee. 2003. Marra Farm hosts Fall Fest October 4. *P-Patch Post* (Fall): 4. Seattle: Friends of P-Patch.

Harper, Lee, and Jen Ferguson. 2002. Growing the right food. . . . to give. *P-Patch Post* (Winter): 6. Seattle: Friends of P-Patch.

Higbee, Eric Steven. 2006. *Seattle's last/first farm: Cultivating community agriculture, and environment in our urban context.* Master's thesis, Department of Landscape Architecture, University of Washington.

Hughes-Jelen, Wendy. 2002. A marriage of plants and people. *P-Patch Post* (Fall): 5. Seattle: Friends of P-Patch.

Jones and Jones Architects and Landscape Architects. 2000. South Park Marra Farm master plan design process, Spring 2000. Text and plans.

Lettuce Link. 2005. Welcome to Lettuce Ink! *Lettuce Ink* 1 (1): 1. http://www.fre-montpublic.org/publications/LL1Q.pdf (accessed April 11, 2007).

———. 2006. Connecting chefs and kids at Marra Farm *Lettuce Ink* 2 (2): 3. http://www.fremontpublic.org/publications/LL1Q4.pdf (accessed April 11, 2007).

———. 2006/2007. Lettuce Link highlights of 2006. *Lettuce Ink* 2 (3): http://www.solid-ground.org/Programs/Nutrition/Lettuce/Pages/default.aspx (accessed October 25, 2007).

Macdonald, Rich. 2004a. News from other P-Patch gardens. *P-Patch Post* (Summer): 5. Seattle: P-Patch Trust.

———. 2004b. News from other P-Patch gardens. *P-Patch Post* (Fall): 4. Seattle: P-Patch Trust.

———. 2005. News from other P-Patch gardens. *P-Patch Post* (Summer): 5. Seattle: P-Patch Trust.

Raymond, Laura. 2000. South Park Marra Farm. *P-Patch Post* (Summer): N.p. Seattle: Friends of P-Patch.

Seattle (City) Department of Neighborhoods. 2005. Marra Farm. http://www.ci.seattle.wa.us/neighborhoods/ppatch/locations/36.htm (accessed June 10, 2005).

Seattle (City of) Parks and Recreation Department. 2006. Marra Farm community project pro parks project information. http://www.ci.seattle.wa.us/parks/

proparks/projects/marrafarm.htm (updated April 5, 2006; accessed April 6, 2006).

———. 2007a. Marra-Desimone Park pro parks project information. http://www. seattle.gov/parks/proparks/projects/Marra-Desimone.htm (updated March 7, 2007; accessed April 11, 2007).

———. 2007b. Community Meeting #2, April 29, 2006. Meeting Notes (PDF), link from Marra Farm community project pro parks project information. http:// www.ci.seattle.wa.us/parks/proparks/projects/marrafarm.htm (updated March 7, 2007; accessed April 11, 2007).

———. 2007c. Community Meeting #3, June 7, 2006. Meeting Notes (PDF), link from Marra Farm community project pro parks project information. http:// www.seattle.gov/parks/proparks/projects/marrafarm.htm (updated March 7, 2007; accessed April 11, 2007).

———. 2007d. Open House/Meeting #4, October 7, 2006. Marra Farm community project pro parks project information. http://www.seattle.gov/parks/proparks/ projects/marrafarm.htm (updated March 7, 2007; accessed April 11, 2007).

Seattle (City of). 2007. Seattle Parks Names 3 Parks in West Seattle and South Seattle. News Advisory (February 20, 2007). http://www.seattlechannel.org/news/ detail.asp?ID=7031&Dept=14 (accessed April 11, 2007).

Seattle Post-Intelligencer. 2006. Georgetown/South Park Census Data. http:// seattlepi.nwsource.com/webtowns/article.asp?WTID=20&ID=107876 (accessed May 11, 2006).

Seattle Youth Garden Works (SYGW). 2005. Marra Farm. http://www.sygw.org/ marra.shtml (accessed August 3, 2005).

Solid Ground. 2007. Marra Farm. http://www.solid-ground.org/Programs/Nutri- tion/Marra/Pages/default.aspx (accessed October 27, 2007).

Washington State University (WSU) King County Extension. 2007. The ninth annual harvest celebration farm tour in King County. http://king.wsu.edu/ foodandfarms/HarvestCelebration.html (accessed October 27, 2007).

Magnuson References

Alexander, Gemma. 2003. There's a P-Patch to fit every style of gardener. *P-Patch Post* (Winter): 3. Seattle: Friends of P-Patch.

Barker Landscape Architects. 2000. Magnuson Community Garden. Submitted to Magnuson Community Garden Committee. August. Part 3. PDF. http://www. seattle.gov/magnusongarden/Report/FRContents.htm (accessed February 11, 2006).

Bergelin, Lynn. 2003 Essay: Too much "community" in a very public garden? *P-Patch Post* (Fall): 5. Seattle: Friends of P-Patch.

DeMerritt, Lynn. 2002. Magnuson Community Garden at Sand Point Magnuson Park (MCG). *P-Patch Post* (Summer): 5. Seattle: Friends of P-Patch.

Macdonald, Rich. 1999/2000. Magnuson Park Community Garden. *P-Patch Post* (Winter): 1.

———. 2001. Site developments. *P-Patch Post* (Fall): 7. Seattle: Friends of P-Patch.

Magnuson Children's Garden. N.d. The Children's Garden. Magnuson Community Garden. Warren G. Magnuson Park. Seattle, WA.

Magnuson Community Garden. 2006a. The P-Patch at Magnuson Community Garden. http://www.cityofseattle.net/magnusongarden/P-Patch/MGP-Patch.htm (accessed February 8, 2006).

———. 2006b. About the Magnuson Community Garden. http://www.ci.seattle. wa.us/magnusongarden/AboutMCG.htm (accessed February 8, 2006).

———. 2006c. Frequently asked questions. http://www.seattle.gov/magnusongarden/MGfaq.htm (accessed February 8, 2006).

———. 2006d. Report of Activities for 2002. http://www.ci.seattle.wa.us/magnusongarden/Report/MGReport2002.htm (accessed February 8, 2006).

———. 2006e. Summary of Phase I: Designing Magnuson Community Garden. http://www.seattle.gov/magnusongarden/History/MGphase1.htm (accessed February 8, 2006).

———. 2006f. Magnuson Garden Design Process. http://www.seattle.gov/magnusongarden/history/MGDesign.htm (accessed February 8, 2006).

———. 2006g. Summary of Activities for 2003. http://www.seattle.gov/magnusongarden/Report/MGReport2003.htm (accessed February 8, 2006).

———. 2006h. Amphitheater in Magnuson Community Garden. http://www.cityofseattle.net/magnusongarden/Amphitheater.htm (accessed February 8, 2006).

———. 2006i. Summary of Phase II: Funding and Construction of Magnuson Community Garden. http://www.seattle.gov/magnusongarden/History/MGphase2.htm (accessed February 8, 2006).

———. 2006j. Recognition of Magnuson Community Garden contributors 2002–2003." http://www.seattle.gov/magnusongarden/donors.htm (accessed February 8, 2006).

———. 2006k. Children's' Garden. http://www.cityofseattle.net/magnusongarden/Child/Childrens.htm (accessed February 8, 2006).

———. 2006l. Magnuson Community Garden Organization. http://www.cityofseattle.gov/magnusongarden/CityRel.htm (accessed February 8, 2006).

———. 2006m. Work Parties and Other Events. Information as of May 30, 2006. http://www.cityofseattle.gov/magnusongarden/MG-party.htm (accessed June 6, 2006).

———. 2006n. Native Plant Nursery. http://www.cityofseattle.net/magnusongarden/Nursery/Nursery.htm (accessed February 8, 2006).

———. 2006o. The Orchard in Magnuson Community Garden. http://www.cityofseattle.net/magnusongarden/Orchard/Orchard.htm (accessed February 8, 2006).

———. 2006p. Planning for Phase 3 Draft—Preliminary Considerations. http://

www.cityofseattle.gov/magnusongarden/MGPlan.htm (accessed February 8, 2006).

Moty, Joyce. 2003. In praise of public spaces. *P-Patch Post* (Winter): 3. Seattle: Friends of P-Patch.

Seattle (City of) Department of Neighborhoods. 2005. "P-patch community gardens Magnuson Park." http://www.ci.seattle.wa.us/neighborhoods/ppatch/locations/7.htm (accessed June 10, 2005).

Seattle (City of) Legislative Information Service. 2008. Resolution Number 30063. http://clerk.ci.seattle.wa.us/%7Escripts/nph-brs.exe?s1=&s2=&s3=30063&s4=&Sect4=AND&l=20&Sect1=IMAGE&Sect2=THESON&Sect3=PLURON&Sect5=RESN1&Sect6=HITOFF&d=RESN&p=1&u=/%7Epublic/resn1.htm&r=1&f=G (updated as of May 4, 2008; accessed May 4, 2008).

Seattle (City of) Parks and Recreation Department. 2006a. Warren G. Magnuson Park. About the Park. http://www.cityofseattle.net/parks/magnuson/vision.htm (updated April 6, 2006; accessed May 12, 2006).

———. 2006b. Warren G. Magnuson Park vision for the 21st century park. http://www.ci.seattle.wa.us/parks/magnuson/vision.htm (updated May 9, 2006; accessed May 16, 2006).

Seattle Post-Intelligencer. 2006. Sand Point Census Data. http://seattlepi.nwsource.com/webtowns/census.asp?WTID=34 (accessed May 11, 2006).

RESOURCES

The following Web sites give greater context to the material presented in this document:

American Community Gardening Association:
http://www.communitygarden.org/

City Farmer, "Urban Agriculture Notes":
http://www.cityfarmer.org/

Community Food Security Coalition:
http://www.foodsecurity.org/

Garden Mosaics:
http://www.gardenmosaics.cornell.edu/

Seattle Market Gardens:
http://www.seattlemarketgardens.org/

Seattle P-Patch Community Gardens:
http://www.ci.seattle.wa.us/neighborhoods/ppatch/

Seattle Youth Garden Works:
http://www.sygw.org/

A NOTE FROM THE LANDSCAPE ARCHITECTURE FOUNDATION

The Landscape Architecture Foundation's Land and Community Design Case Study Series consists of analytical publications by contemporary scholars and practitioners about topical issues and actual places in which design offers holistic solutions to economic, social, and environmental challenges. Its goal is to provide a legacy of rigorous, in-depth research and critical thinking that will advance enlightened planning and development in the classroom, in practice, and in policy.

LAF gratefully acknowledges direct support for the series from the following sponsors: the JJR Research Fund, which supports applied research that explores the complex interrelationship of social, physical, economic and environmental forces that comprise sustainable design and development; the CLASS Fund Ralph Hudson Environmental Fellowship, which supports research in landscape change, preservation and stewardship, and the connection between people and landscapes; and the AILA Yamagami Hope Fellowship. The William Penn Foundation, which is dedicated to efforts that deepen connections to nature and community, also provided support to the series.

Additionally, ongoing, generous support to LAF and its programs is provided by the American Society of Landscape Architects, whose mission is "to lead, to educate, and to participate in the careful stewardship, wise planning, and artful design of our cultural and natural environments."

Major support for LAF is also provided by EDSA, Landscape Forms, EDAW, Landscape Structures, L. M. Scofield Company, Peridian International, Burton Landscape Architecture Studio + Gallery, the HOK Planning Group, and the SWA Group.

Lead donors include ah'bé landscape architects; an anonymous donor, in appreciation of ASLA past president Perry Howard; Chip Crawford; Mark Dawson; Economic Research Associates; Graham Landscape Architecture; HGOR Planners & Landscape Architects; Hunter Industries; Bill Main; OLIN; Lucinda Reed Sanders; and Sitecraft.

The list of additional donors who provide generous and sustained funding is too lengthy to include, but their support is invaluable to LAF and its programs.

INDEX